Modern *memory* Keeper

A *new* approach to scrapbooking your family legacy

by Ronee Parsons

Memory Makers Books
Cincinnati, Ohio
www.mycraftivity.com

12 11 10 09 08   5 4 3 2 1

Distributed in Canada by Fraser Direct
100 Armstrong Avenue
Georgetown, ON, Canada L7G 5S4
Tel: (905) 877-4411

Distributed in the U.K. and Europe by David & Charles
Brunel House, Newton Abbot, Devon, TQ12 4PU, England
Tel: (+44) 1626 323200, Fax: (+44) 1626 323319
E-mail: postmaster@davidandcharles.co.uk

Distributed in Australia by Capricorn Link
P.O. Box 704, S. Windsor, NSW 2756 Australia
Tel: (02) 4577-3555

Library of Congress Cataloging-in-Publication Data
Parsons, Ronee.
   modern memory keeper / Ronee Parsons. -- 1st ed.
      p. cm.
   Includes bibliographical references and index.
   ISBN-13: 978-1-59963-019-9 (pbk. : alk. paper)
   1. Photograph albums.
   2. Photographs--Conservation and restoration.
   3. Scrapbooks. I. Title.
TR501.P37 2008
745.593--dc22
                        2008001098

Metric Conversion Chart

to convert	to	multiply by
Inches	Centimeters	2.54
Centimeters	Inches	0.4
Feet	Centimeters	30.5
Centimeters	Feet	0.03
Yards	Meters	0.9
Meters	Yards	1.1
Sq. Inches	Sq. Centimeters	6.45
Sq. Centimeters	Sq. Inches	0.16
Sq. Feet	Sq. Meters	0.09
Sq. Meters	Sq. Feet	10.8
Sq. Yards	Sq. Meters	0.8
Sq. Meters	Sq. Yards	1.2
Pounds	Kilograms	0.45
Kilograms	Pounds	2.2
Ounces	Grams	28.3
Grams	Ounces	0.035

Editor: Amy Glander
Designers: Corrie Schaffeld, Jeremy Werling
Art Coordinator: Eileen Aber
Production Coordinator: Matt Wagner
Photographers: Al Parrish, Christine Polomsky
Stylists: Nora Martini, Jan Nickum

F+W PUBLICATIONS, INC.

www.fwpublications.com

dedication

This book is dedicated to my husband, Eric, for encouraging me to follow my heart and be true to myself, and, most of all, for joining me to create a new family of our own.

Love you always.

acknowledgments

Thank you, thank you, thank you...

... to the companies who generously donated their beautiful products: American Crafts, Cherry Arte, Everlasting Keepsakes, Fancy Pants Designs, Gel-a-tins, Hambly Screen Prints, Heidi Swapp, Prima Marketing, Ranger, SEI, The Crafter's Workshop and WorldWin Papers.

... to my talented contributing artists: Karen Bowers, Erin Derkatz, Catherine Feegel-Erhardt, Lana Rappette, Cindy Ellen Russell, Katrina Simeck and Michele Skinner. Thanks for taking the time to share your art with me and the world.

... to Crystal Jeffrey Rieger for not only contributing artwork, but for also helping me develop the concept of this book and seeing it through to fruition. Thanks for walking with me on this journey.

... to Christine Doyle and the staff at Memory Makers for their encouragement and support.

... to my family for digging through their old photos and enthusiastically answering my incessant questions.

... and to Eric and Elvis for supporting me throughout this project. I couldn't have done it without you.

how
to
name

a
grandparent

of other family
nonsense

Contents

A Modern Approach...

When I first began scrapbooking, I went to my basement and pulled out a few boxes of photos that had been sitting there for what seemed like forever. I organized them one by one in chronological order, and then began the heavy task of scrapping all of them...in order. At some point it dawned on me that this wasn't fun. My pages were uninspired and portrayed nothing more than if I had just shoved them into a pre-made photo album.

That's when I realized family is not about names and dates, memories are not chronological and my artistic expression was just as important to the page as the photo itself. So I started over. I began again with a new goal—to scrap my family's stories, to scrap my family's personalities and to scrap my family's traditions. My heritage comprises more than mundane details like names, dates and numbers, and so does yours.

It's the quirky everyday moments, memories and personalities, like an old song by Jim Reeves or homemade ice cream hand-cranked in a wooden barrel, that make our families unique and interesting. I challenge you to scrap your family's stories, personalities and traditions in a way that inspires you. Toss the rules of heritage scrapbooking out the window and begin again fresh. Look to the amazing examples in the pages that follow for inspiration on new ways to keep your family memories rich and colorful.

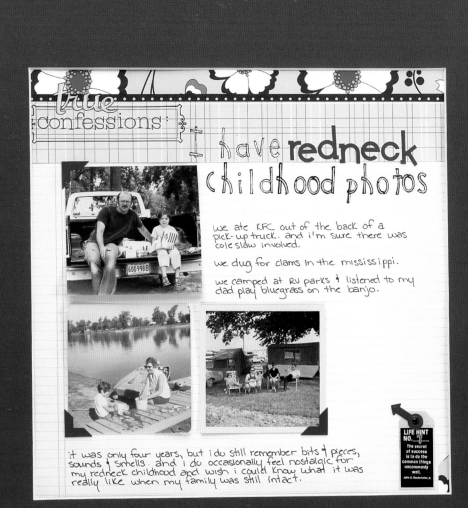

Telling Your Family's Story

As I'm sitting here writing this, I'm watching *Casablanca*, my all-time favorite film. If you haven't seen it, go now. (Yes, I'm giving you permission to put down the book, but only for a moment!) I'm sitting with a cup of tea, my journal and a good pen, pondering what it is that makes this movie so classic. Is it the image of Humphrey Bogart smoking his cigarette? Is it Ingrid Bergman's arresting beauty? Is it nostalgia for another time? These things are important details, but the real reason *Casablanca* has become a classic for me is that it captures the personal side of a piece of the world's history, an amazing story of living and loving in a time of political turmoil. It gets right to the root of the characters and their relationships. This is what you should try to accomplish with your heritage pages and albums. The things that make your family special are not lists of places, names and dates. The things that make your family memorable are the irreplaceable recipes your grandmother has passed down since the Great War, the story your grandfather tells about when he escaped across the border, that opal pendant that's been worn by every generation of women in your family since the 1700s. Your family's personality is in the details. It is up to you to find them.

Find the stories in your family history and capture them on your page. This is the essence of who you are. This is the essence of who your children will be. Live it, document it and love it.

Keep a Family Journal

There are so many stories that make up a family history, sometimes it can become overwhelming to try to document them all. Start simple. Buy a blank journal. Anything will do, as long as it is small enough to carry with you in your purse or shoulder bag. Get yourself a good pen to go along with it. I like to use one that clips directly on the cover or spiral binding. Begin taking this journal to all family gatherings. Write down stories, thoughts, quotes or observations of anything related to your family. Where people lived, what their houses were like, childhood memories, birth stories, wedding stories, war stories. When something comes up—an anecdote, the seed of a story—ask questions. Get your family members talking. You'll notice that once they start, they won't want to stop and before you know it, you'll have plenty of material to begin completing your first pages.

The next time you are at a family gathering, pull out your family journal and write down those stories that are told at every event. You know the ones you've heard a thousand times. The ones that grow more extravagant in details each time they are told. It wouldn't be a family get-together without them, and it certainly wouldn't be a family heritage album without them. I call these stories "Tall Tales," and although they might not be entirely true, they represent the mythology of your family, part of the glue that holds your tribe together. Gather these stories together in a fun mini album.

This mini album is so quick and easy, it is perfect for recording family stories when your journal gets a bit full. This album can be made in any standard photo size. Here, I've used 5" x 7" (13cm x 18cm), but you could also use 2" x 3" (5cm x 8cm), 4" x 6" (10cm x 15cm), or 8" x 10" (20cm x 25cm).

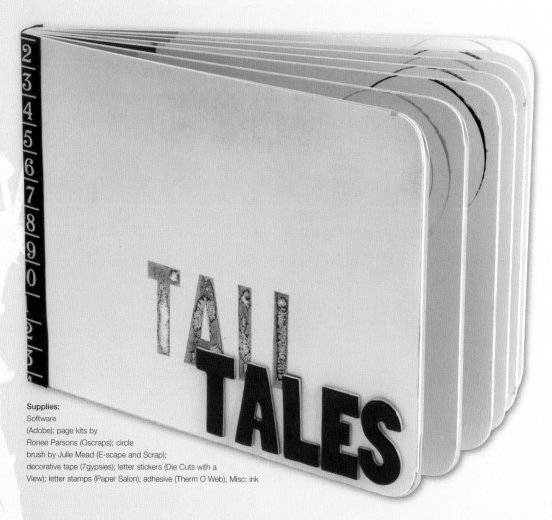

Supplies:
Software
(Adobe); page kits by
Ronee Parsons (Oscraps); circle
brush by Julie Mead (E-scape and Scrap);
decorative tape (7gypsies); letter stickers (Die Cuts with a
View); letter stamps (Paper Salon); adhesive (Therm O Web); Misc: ink

Tall Tales

a collection of silly stories
that make up your family tree.

For Elvis,
Love Mama

Include a short title page at the beginning of your mini book to introduce album-gazers to the collection of stories they will see. Think about who will view this album. Is it for you, your child or other family members? Write your journaling with your audience in mind. I dedicated this album to my son and wrote my journaling in a voice and tone he could relate to and enjoy.

Poor Auntie Trina came home
from college because her heart had been
broken. She was so upset that she could hardly stand it.

Grandma Knoche took Trina
out to pick cherries and then baked her a very
special cherry pie. The two of them went out shopping and left
the pie to cool. The cherry pie was the only thing she had
to look forward to that evening.

Meanwhile Papa Rich came home and
found a fresh-baked cherry pie in the fridge.
He decided to help himself to the whole thing!
He didn't even leave a crumb for Aunt Trina. The only thing
left was a dirty pie plate.

Cherry Pi

Photo: Thom Wall

If you don't have a photo that matches a story you've recorded in your family journal, search online for stock photographs that might work. Many stock photography sites offer photos free (or almost free) for personal use. Check iStockphoto (www.istockphoto.com), stock.xchng (www.sxc.hu) or LuckyOliver (www.luckyoliver.com), or simply Google (www.google.com) the term "stock photos." Be aware of copyright law as it applies to stock photography and be sure to credit the original photographer if you're going to have the photo published in print or online.

In sixth grade Grandma Shawnee had an admirerer. She thought he was a dork, but he thought she was wonderful. So wonderful, in fact, that he named his pet lizard Shawnee after her.

One day he brought the lizard to school for show-and-tell. He snuck up behind Grandma and placed the lizard right on her shoulder.

Grandma freaked! She started screaming, and ran away, but the lizard fell from her shoulder. She stepped right on it and the tail came off.

The boy didn't think she was so wonderful after that.

Lizard's Tails

Forget all the rules you think you know about creating heritage albums and pages. Combine stories that feel right together. For this album I combined stories from both sides of my family and many different generations. Mix it up a little; you never know what you'll come up with!

When Grandpa Dan was about seven and Uncle Shawn was three the two of them wandered down to the laundromat at their apartments. Grandpa Dan put Shawn in one of the washing machines so that he could pretend like he was on TV.

Then Grandpa decided he wanted to be on TV too. He made Uncle Shawn get out so that he could climb in. Shawn shut the door and Grandpa did his television impersonation. But when he was done, Shawn couldn't get the door open. They were a mile from their apartment and Shawn was only three years old!

Grandpa Dan remembers yelling "Go get Dad! Go get Dad!" Shawn left and Grandpa thought for sure he would be stuck forever. But three hours later Shawn appeared dragging Great Grandpa Dan by the hand.

On TV

Photo: Geerah Baden

Just because a story is old doesn't mean the photo has to be. Pictures of places that make up the setting of a story are wonderful substitutions if you can't find an appropriate photo. Remember, sometimes the laundromat can be just as interesting as the Louvre. Another idea is to re-enact a scene with your own children and use that to scrap. Take them to the scene of one of your family stories and bring your camera along. You'll capture great photos for your family heritage pages and probably make a few new memories while you're at it.

Tacos and Noses

When Mama was about six, and Uncle Danny was about one and a half, we all sat down at dinner for tacos and chocolate milk.

As we ate, Uncle Danny began to sneeze. At first it was just a couple of sneezes, but soon he couldn't stop. He sneezed and sneezed and sneezed! Finally Grandma and Grandpa decided they should take him to the hospital to see what was wrong.

At the hospital the doctor took a small flashlight to look up Danny's nose. It was packed with taco meat! He took out a giant set of tweezers and had to pick out the taco meat piece by piece. The doctor said it was the grossest thing he had ever seen.

Generate a common theme or idea for your album. It can be anything from fairy tales passed down through generations, songs your family sings on special occasions or sweet childhood memories. Think outside the box!

creative *sparks*

When creating a heritage album, don't feel like you have to capture everything all at once. Take a moment to think of the stories that you would like to tell and what they have in common. That's all it takes to create a wonderful theme for an album. Here are a few more ideas to spark that creative genius.

- *Create an album based on the events of one family member's life. Think of it as a biography. Get stories from as many people who knew your subject as possible and gather photos from throughout his or her life.*

- *Choose a theme for an album chronicling the stories that accompany events that recur in every family. For instance, gather together all of the wedding stories or birth stories into one album.*

- *Make a gift album for a friend based on his or her family history. Talk to family members to gather stories and photos. Then, do some research into the history of his or her family name. The Internet is a great place to start a search like this.*

- *Choose a period of time, such as the first few years after your family migrated to a new country, or a time when part of the family was stationed overseas, and collect as many photos and stories as you can from that era.*

- *Gather together stories and photos from one generation and create an album based on that information and ephemera. Include stories of growing up, births, marriages and where those family members are now.*

Tell the Story

Sometimes too much information makes it just as difficult to journal on your pages as not enough. There are many ways to tell a story. I find it easier to finalize my journaling before I write it on the page. Play around with different ways of telling the same story and choose the one that best suits the mood of your page.

Grouping text into list format is a wonderful way to tell a story. It keeps the journaling quick and light and the viewer's focus on the feeling inspired by the photo and the mood of the layout. You can list pretty much anything, and you don't necessarily have to focus on tangible items. Try brainstorming on a blank sheet of paper to come up with a unique angle for the story you are telling. List different parts of the story and see if any of them inspire the mood you are seeking for your page. This will also help you get in the habit of thinking about the tiny details that give life to a memory.

Artwork: Lana Rappette

Journaling in list format can be as simple as drawing attention to an article of clothing a relative was known for wearing, a phrase he said often or an activity she enjoyed. Strengthen your list with a series of photos.

Supplies: Cardstock (Bazzill); patterned paper (Prima); chipboard accents (Li'l Davis, Maya Road, We R Memory Keepers); die-cuts (SEI); ribbon (Deja Views, May Arts, Prima); rub-ons (Hambly); adhesive (Aleene's, EK Success, Tombow); Misc: acrylic paint, edge distresser, glitter, pen

Selective coloring is an excellent way to draw attention to a specific part of a photo. It can be done digitally (look for tutorials for your software online) or by using a paint pen or colored pencil. Always order doubles when you have photos printed so you can write or color on them without fear you will ruin your only copy.

Artwork: Catherine Feegel-Erhardt

With a funky twist on the usual portrayal of a family tree, Catherine uses a list to express one of her mother's greatest accomplishments—mothering. Try to use listing in an untraditional format like this one to turn often mundane genealogical facts like names and dates into a celebration of a relative's life.

Supplies: Cardstock (Bazzill); patterned paper, rub-ons, transparency (Hambly); chipboard (EK Success); decorative tape, transparent letters (Heidi Swapp); rhinestones (Heidi Swapp); tag (Innovative Storage); stamps (Inkadinkado, Little Black Dress); adhesives (EK Success, Ranger, Therm O Web); Misc: eyelet, ink, paint, staples, thread

- tree House
- TO BUILD A
- You need....
- A good tree.
- One used car-seat dragged from a local scrap-yard. and
- a brother.
- Richard and Tommy Sampson

Simple memories often portray a larger story of a family relationship. Don't pass over a perfectly wonderful photo just because it doesn't capture a momentous event. Use a list to journal simple yet poignant family memories.

Supplies: Cardstock (WorldWin); patterned paper (Bo-Bunny); letter sticker (Arctic Frog); letters, tags (Heidi Swapp); flowers (American Crafts); adhesive (Therm O Web); ink (Ranger)

Making Creative Journaling Strips

Journaling strips are an easy way to add your list to a layout without adding bulk. They also allow you to be creative with how and where you place each line of journaling.

Begin by speaking with a person who is one of the main subjects in the photo, or someone close to them, to find out the story. Ask questions about what they were doing, who they were with, if the activity was a regular event or something out of the ordinary, and anything else you can think of. Take notes in your family journal, and then form a list from the details that stand out most.

Materials

- Cardstock
- Paper trimmer or scissors
- Ink pad (any color)
- Archival pen

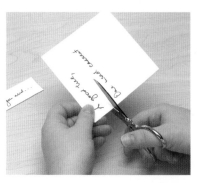

1 Choose four to six of the details and write them on a coordinating color of cardstock using an archival pen. Be sure to leave space between each detail for cutting.

2 Cut apart the details into small strips or chunks.

3 Rub the edges of the journal strips across your ink pad. For a clean definition, be careful to touch only the edges to the cardstock. For a more distressed and textured look, allow the pad to touch further into the strip.

First Person

Writing in first person means to write the way you normally write your everyday thoughts and comments from your own perspective. Use "I" statements such as "I saw this..." or "I felt this..." when writing in a first-person voice. This is an excellent choice when you would like to share as much about your experience gathering the information as you would the information itself, and it is probably the type of journaling that will flow most naturally.

Artwork: Katrina Simeck

Here, Katrina uses first person journaling to share details she remembers about her grandmother's house. The specific sights, sounds and smells she describes give this layout a warm and comfortable feeling.

Supplies: Cardstock (Bazzill); patterned paper (BasicGrey, Fancy Pants); letter stickers, rub-ons (American Crafts); chipboard (Scenic Route); flower (Heidi Swapp); journal card, lace (Fancy Pants); adhesive (Duck); Misc: pen

true confessions: I have **redneck** childhood photos

we ate KFC out of the back of a pick-up truck. and i'm sure there was cole slaw involved.

we dug for clams in the mississippi.

we camped at RV parks & listened to my dad play bluegrass on the banjo.

it was only four years, but i do still remember bits & pieces, sounds & smells. and i do occasionally feel nostalgic for my redneck childhood and wish i could know what it was really like when my family was still intact.

LIFE HINT NO. _7_
The secret of success is to do the common things uncommonly well.
John D. Rockefeller, Jr.

Artwork: Michele Skinner

Don't forget to record your own childhood. Photos of you with your parents are just as important as older photos and stories. Your children will appreciate that you've preserved your thoughts and recollections, and so will you. First-person journaling is an excellent way to tell your own stories of your family and what memories certain photos bring to mind.

Supplies: Patterned paper (American Crafts, Piggy Tales, Scenic Route); letter stickers (Creative Imaginations, KI Memories); accents (7gypsies); rub-ons (American Crafts); stamps (Fontwerks); adhesive (3M, Tombow); Misc: pen

creative*sparks*

Brainstorm details about people and places before writing your journaling. If you didn't know the person or the place, ask a family member to brainstorm for you. If you can almost smell the fresh-baked cookies and see the orange shag carpet, then generations to come will be able to experience these sensory details through your journaling.

It's great to see pics of my dad at this age. I love the wonder & excitement in his eyes. In this picture he was only about six. The family was living on a base at the time, in military housing. Dad always told us the story of how he could often hear a man's voice and footsteps near the door of their house. He would often get up to go see if Grandpa was home only to find that he was still alone. I've always enjoyed hearing his memories from that time.
–Rome
05/01/09

To add an even more personal touch to your first-person journaling, hand-draw your journaling lines and add doodling. It can be scary at first to write directly onto a layout. If you are nervous, you can always try journaling on cardstock and adding that to the page, but think of how wonderful it would be if you found a letter from your great grandmother written in her own hand. You wouldn't care if it was messy!

Supplies: Patterned paper, tags (Prima, SEI); letters (Heidi Swapp); doodle template (Crafter's Workshop); adhesive (Therm O Web); Misc: acrylic paint, pen

Using a Doodling Template

A doodling template is a no-fear way to add the personal feeling of hand-drawn graphics and journaling lines to a layout. Doodling templates come in many different patterns and shapes. I like to use ones that leave some open space in the design for me to customize the drawing.

Materials

- Cardstock
- Doodling template
- Poster tape
  (or other removable tape)
- Archival pen

1   Adhere a sheet of cardstock to your work surface with poster tape.

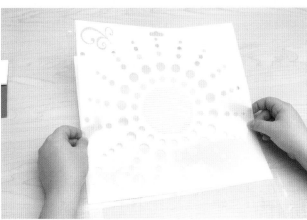

2   Position the doodling template over the cardstock as desired. Attach it to the work surface at the corners.

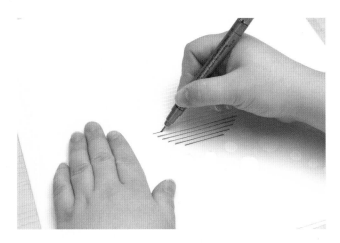

3   Carefully draw inside the template onto the cardstock as desired. Remove the template and journal on the journaling lines.

Third Person

Writing in third person removes you from the story. When writing in third person you become the narrator, using statements like "He did this..." or "She felt this way...". This is a more formal style of writing, and it can take a little bit of practice. But when used correctly, it can have excellent results.

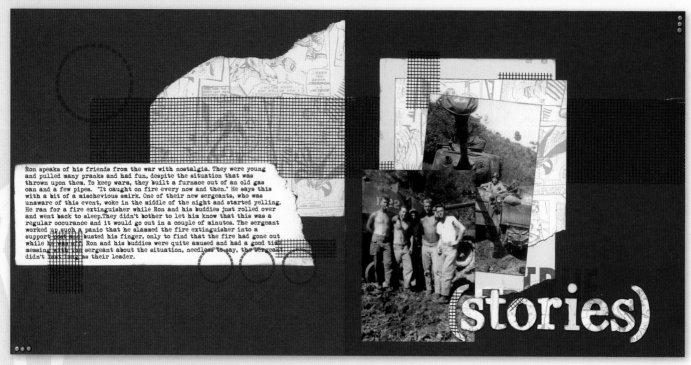

On this page I used third-person journaling so that I could share my grandfather's stories objectively. When writing in third person, think of yourself as a narrator speaking to an audience. This will help you remove yourself from the story so your own opinions and perceptions won't alter it.

Supplies: Cardstock (WorldWin); patterned paper (Arctic Frog, Sandylion); letter stamps (Paper Salon); chipboard letters (Zsiage); stamps (Sugarloaf); mesh (Magic Mesh); adhesive (Therm O Web); Misc: brads, ink

Using third person is also an excellent way to reflect on what a relative was like before you knew him or her and how that differs from the person he or she is today. For this layout, Lana used a casual voice in third person to describe the way her grandmother was early in life and how that is different from the "Grandma" she is now. Using third person doesn't have to be stiff and boring; it just takes the "I" out of the writing. With a little bit of practice, you'll have this style down in no time.

Supplies: Cardstock, brad, flower (Bazzill); patterned paper (BasicGrey, Fiskars, Heidi Grace, Prima); chipboard letter (Li'l Davis); doodling template (Crafter's Workshop); transparent dot (Cloud 9); rub-ons (Autumn Leaves, Luxe Designs); adhesive (Aleene's, Tombow); Misc: ink, pen

Artwork: Lana Rappette

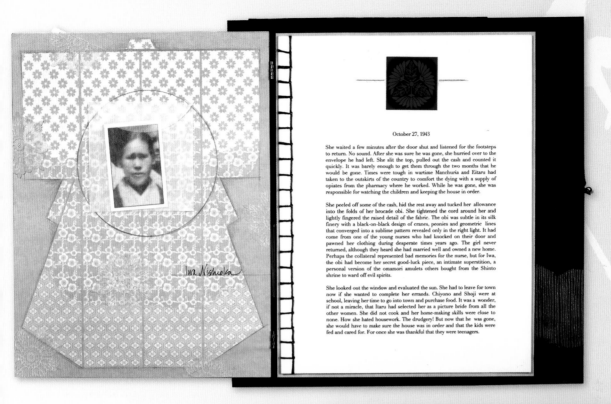

October 27, 1943

She waited a few minutes after the door shut and listened for the footsteps to return. No sound. After she was sure he was gone, she hurried over to the envelope he had left. She slit the top, pulled out the cash and counted it quickly. It was barely enough to get them through the two months that he would be gone. Times were tough in wartime Manchuria and Eitaru had taken to the outskirts of the country to comfort the dying with a supply of opiates from the pharmacy where he worked. While he was gone, she was responsible for watching the children and keeping the house in order.

She peeled off some of the cash, hid the rest away and tucked her allowance into the folds of her brocade obi. She tightened the cord around her and lightly fingered the raised detail of the fabric. The obi was subtle in its silk finery with a black-on-black design of cranes, peonies and geometric lines that converged into a sublime pattern revealed only in the right light. It had come from one of the young nurses who had knocked on their door and pawned her clothing during desperate times years ago. The girl never returned, although they heard she had married well and owned a new home. Perhaps the collateral represented bad memories for the nurse, but for Iwa, the obi had become her secret good-luck piece, an intimate superstition, a personal version of the omamori amulets others bought from the Shinto shrine to ward off evil spirits.

She looked out the window and evaluated the sun. She had to leave for town now if she wanted to complete her errands. Chiyono and Shoji were at school, leaving her time to go into town and purchase food. It was a wonder, if not a miracle, that Itaru had selected her as a picture bride from all the other women. She did not cook and her home-making skills were close to none. How she hated housework. The drudgery! But now that he was gone, she would have to make sure the house was in order and that the kids were fed and cared for. For once she was thankful that they were teenagers.

Third person can also give you the freedom to share family stories that are sometimes difficult to get objective information about. By taking feelings and opinions out of the story, you are free to tell the whole story. Not all family stories are happy ones, but that doesn't mean they shouldn't be recorded or shared. Third-person journaling can help you remove yourself from the story or situation and therefore share details on a layout that you may not have otherwise.

Supplies: Cardstock (Bazzill, Paper Accents); patterned paper (Cavallini, Kodomo, SEI); chipboard, letters (Li'l Davis, Making Memories); brad, hinges (Making Memories); stamps (Making Memories, Plaid, Sugarloaf); stickers (Midori); tag, twill (Rusty Pickle); transparency (My Mind's Eye); Misc: chalk, colored pencils, ink, pen, wax

Artwork: Cindy Ellen Russell

Tell the Story with Pictures

Sometimes you may have a stack of pictures that tell a great story all on their own. When this happens, you can allow the pictures to speak for themselves. Combine multiple photos on a one- or two-page layout to create a photo collage. Choose a title based on where the picture was taken or the name of the relative in the photos (if you know it) and let the combination of pictures and your color choices convey the rest of the story.

Combine groups of photos to portray the stories of different parts of your family. Here, I've combined photos of my grandmother when she was young with photos of her sisters, parents and grandparents. I like that through the combination of photos you can begin to feel what it was like to be a part of the Frazier family at that time, and what it may have been like to know them. Use this method for groups of pictures that, individually, don't have a story, but together show a greater piece of your family history.

Supplies: Software (Adobe); digital brads, frame, letters by Ronee Parsons (Oscraps); background paper by Dana Frantz (Scrapbook Graphics); swirl, wings by Karen Auken (E-Scape and Scrap)

Artwork: Michele Skinner

Another way to tell a story with photos is to choose a similar photo of successive generations and combine them together on the same page. You may not be lucky enough to have a photo where each generation is in the same pose, but try to choose photos that have similar moods, then choose colors and patterns that enhance those moods.

Supplies: Cardstock (Bazzill); patterned paper, rub-ons (Heidi Grace); letter stickers (American Crafts): chipboard (Die Cuts with a View, Technique Tuesday); adhesives (3M, Tomobow); Misc: paint, pen

Including a variety of different types of photographs about one person will also help portray his or her story. Choose a close-up, a photo of the setting (in film this is called an establishing shot) and at least one candid photo. Creating a grouping of photos like the one here, along with your choice of colors and patterns, will give the viewer an instant feel for who your relative was.

Supplies: Cardstock (Bazzill, Prima); patterned paper (Die Cuts with a View, Hambly); rub-ons (Hambly, Melissa Frances); stamps (Fancy Pants, My Sentiments Exactly); stickers (K&Co.); transparency (My Mind's Eye); adhesive (Aleene's, EK Success, Tombow); Misc: embossing powder, ink, pen, ribbon

Artwork: Lana Rappette

Combine multiple photos on a page to make use of photos that wouldn't otherwise be able to carry a layout on their own. Here, Erin moves us through the entire story of her parents' wedding day from the church filling with guests, to the ceremony, all the way through to the happy couple at the reception. Most of these photos are too small and obscure to use on their own, but together they tell a touching story.

Supplies: Cardstock (Scrapbook Sally); patterned paper (Fancy Pants, handmade Batik); decorative tape (Making Memories); transparency (Hambly); Misc: ink, pen

Artwork: Erin Derkatz

Chapter two

Finding Your Family's Story

The most difficult decision on any journey is where to start. Beginning the quest for finding information about your family can be quite daunting. The good news is you don't need to pin down every single branch of your entire family tree to get started. Start with what you know. Document the memories and stories you remember from growing up. Start with the tangible. Search through old books and Bibles for handwritten notes, dedications and stray pieces of paper. Start with communication. Speak to older relatives, ask questions, make phone calls and write letters. Most important, follow where your heart guides you. This story is your story after all. In seeking out your family history, you will find you learn a lot about yourself. Give yourself plenty of time for this journey. Be thorough in your research and use your scrapbook projects as a way to get to know your relatives a bit better.

Talk It Up!

Obviously, the best place to start is close to home. Who knows your family better than, well, your family members, of course? If you've already started keeping a family journal, then you are on the right track. Start asking questions whenever you have the chance. Keep your journal close by, and you'll be amazed with how quickly you begin to fill up the pages.

In a photo like this one, there isn't a whole lot you can tell about the story by just looking at the photo. This picture tells us nothing of who these people were and what they did on a daily basis. Use photos like this one as an opportunity to ask questions about what may have been happening in your relatives' lives at the time the photo was taken.

Supplies: Cardstock (WorldWin); patterned paper (Prima, Urban Lily); transparency (Hambly); stamps (Paper Salon); adhesive (Duck, Therm O Web); Misc: ink, pen

As you begin to fill up your journal full of conversation from family members, you'll find you quickly amass many quotes that give insight into the personalities and dynamics of your family. Capture these little tidbits by adding small quotes or an entire conversation to your scrapbook page.

Supplies: Flowers, patterned paper (American Crafts, Prima); letter stickers, rub-ons (American Crafts, Arctic Frog); ink (Ranger)

Add an extra kick of color to your layouts by inking the edges of patterned papers and cardstocks with distress ink, which comes in a variety of colors.

Artwork: Crystal Jeffrey Rieger

Crystal sat down with her mother and aunt to go through old photos to find their stories. Their reaction to this photo was so strong it warranted a scrapbook page all its own. The way in which our relatives respond to photos, happy or sad, laughing or crying, gives insight into what the individual or time in their life pictured meant to them. Remember to include these impressions in your journal as well.

Supplies: Patterned paper (My Mind's Eye, Scenic Route); number stickers (American Crafts); ribbon (Michaels); adhesives (Scrapbook Adhesive by 3L); Misc: pen

If you have trouble getting some of your relatives to start talking, ask them to write down their stories instead. Using their words to tell their story can be powerful, especially when combined with stunning art.

Supplies: Cardstock (Bazzill); patterned paper, vellum (Kodomo); letter stickers (Making Memories); brads (Karen Foster); die cuts (Creative Imaginations, Fancy Pants); glitter (Ranger); adhesive (Aleene's, EK Success, Tombow); Misc: ink, pen

Artwork: Lana Rappette

Investigate

Once you've gotten people talking, start investigating. This is where you'll need to be a bit creative. I've found that many of my family members sometimes don't divulge information because they assume it's something I'd find boring, when usually it's quite the opposite. Sometimes you really have to do some digging. Start looking through old books. Often you will find handwritten notes in the front cover or tucked between pages. You can often find an entire record of information in the back of an old family Bible. Yearbooks are a wonderful way to find out what a relative was like in his or her younger years. Be creative.

Artwork: Catherine Feegel-Erhardt

Start by paying close attention to the details in photos; you may find you recognize certain elements, like a piece of jewelry or a street sign. While scrapping this page, Catherine noticed the bracelet around her young grandmother's wrist. This bracelet is hers now, and her grandmother asked Catherine to pass it to her daughter. In studying this picture, Catherine was able to remember details about her relationship with her Gram that she can now pass on to her children through her pages. Study photos of relatives when they were young for clues to things that were important to them, and combine what you find with your own memories for a truly touching page.

Supplies: Patterned paper, rub-ons (Hambly); decorative tape (Heidi Swapp); rhinestones (Heidi Swapp, Me & My Big Ideas); adhesive (EK Success)

Write a Letter

Sometimes you'll find that you have to venture outside your immediate family to find the information you are looking for. This is when you can turn to good old-fashioned letter writing. Using a letter to approach distant relatives has many advantages. First, it gives you the chance to introduce yourself without sounding like a salesperson on the phone. Second, it gives your relatives a bit of time to mull over your request and dig through their records before they get back to you. Plus, it's fun to write letters!

Begin by stating who you are and why you are contacting them. Be specific about what you are looking for to ensure they will reply with useful information. Also include a large pre-stamped, self-addressed manila envelope to make it easy for your relatives to respond. Include copies of any research or information you've found up to this point to share with them and to get them excited to do some digging for you.

Artwork: Katrina Simeck

Use the letters you receive back from family members as your journaling. Katrina used an e-mail from her mother for the journaling on this page. This option adds more personality to finished albums because the reader is able to experience memories and stories from more than one source. If you don't have the story in the storyteller's original penmanship, use a font that resembles handwriting to print the journaling.

Supplies: Cardstock (Bazzill); patterned paper (Daisy D's); chipboard heart (Heidi Swapp); digital notepaper, photo overlay by Shabby Princess (Shabby Shoppe); rub-ons (Die Cuts with a View); stamps (Fontwerks); sticker (Making Memories); adhesive (Duck); Misc: brads, ink

creative*sparks*

If you are writing to someone in another country, you can purchase international postage coupons to include in your package. Your relatives will be able to take the coupons in to their local post office and exchange them for the necessary postage to respond to you.

Of course, an entire layout could be about the letter itself. Think about how much insight you get into your relatives' lives by seeing what they find important to include, the type of language they use, how they close their letters and even what their handwriting looks like. Letters, like photos, are little windows into the past and should definitely be included in your pages whenever possible.

Supplies: Cardstock (WorldWin); patterned paper (K&Co.); letter stickers, rub-ons (American Crafts); adhesive (Scrapbook Adhesive by 3L); Misc: pen, staples

Artwork: Crystal Jeffrey Rieger

creative *techniques*

Scanning a letter to include handwriting on a layout

Often it's not possible to include an original letter or note on a scrapbook page, but thanks to technology it's easy to scan these treasures.

1. Scan your note or letter at 300 dpi or greater and then open it in image-editing software.
2. Adjust the image size to fit your layout.
3. Print onto cardstock if you are creating a traditional paper layout. Continue with the following steps for a digital layout.
4. Select the white area of your image using the Magic Wand tool, or make sure your foreground color is set to white and in the tool bar go to Select --> Color Range (with a value of 100).
5. Invert the selection. Select --> Invert
6. Copy the selection. <Ctrl + C>
7. Open a new document with a transparent background and paste the handwritten note on it.
8. Move the handwriting onto a digital layout.

Dear Sping,

The two different poses of the three brothers (PTB, HAB & NAB) were taken in July 1909 on a hunting trip to Laytonville (Mendocino County) while we were staying at Mitchell Ranch. Two chaps with the whiskers were the Mitchell brothers, Mrs. Mitchell (cook) stood behind her husband.

This was before the days of the timed-automatic shutter release, but we had fixed up a long tube to an atomizer bulb that would trip the shutter OK. Note bulb in NAB's right hand in both these pictures. In one picture the rubber tube can be seen passing over the hat in front of Frank.

All good wishes to you both,

Uncle Nate
AKA NAB

Hunting Trip

Artwork: Karen Bowers

If you are lucky enough to have information that a family member has gathered before you, don't hesitate to scrap with the letters he or she has collected as well. Every tidbit of information that you can get your hands on is worth saving and sharing. Here, Karen has used a letter written by one of the subjects in the photo to his niece as her journaling.

Supplies: Software (Adobe); digital patterned paper by Sausan Designs (Scrapbook Graphics); brushes by Kim Liddiard (Digital Scrapbook Place)

When searching for original letters and notes from relatives for your layouts, be sure to also look for writing on the backs of photos, notes at the bottom of jewelry boxes, etc. Anything you can find that will add a missing piece to the puzzle is worth saving.

Supplies: Software (Adobe); digital cardstock by Shabby Princess (Shabby Shoppe); patterned paper by Jessica Bolton (Scrapbook Graphics) and Winggefluester Designs (Oscraps); paper tear by Steph Krush (Digital Paper Tearing); doodles by Ida (Catscrap); frame, tie by Lie Fhung (Ztampf); labels by Vicki Stegall (Oscraps); ribbon by Doris Castle (Scrapbook Graphics)

We had a lot of fun taking care of you. Geo taught Opal & Oma to walk. Opal and Oma at the American Fruit Orchards at Orondo Geo & I were taking care of you Janet in back ground

-Aunt Erma

Artwork: Lana Rappette

Old love notes make excellent embellishments for heritage pages. There are endless ways to include them. You can make them the focus of the page, or fold them and tuck them into a small pocket the way Lana did here. Either way, a handwritten love note is a perfect way to tell the story of a happy couple in love.

Supplies: Cardstock; patterned paper (7gypsies, Creative Imaginations, Kodomo); button (Autumn Leaves); flowers (Petaloo); ribbon (May Arts); stamp (Fontwerks); tag (Making Memories); adhesive (Aleene's, EK Success, Tombow); Misc: ink, pen, rhinestones

You can also turn a layout into a letter itself. On this page, Erin chose to share a part of her personality with her daughter using a combination of photos, words and art. Now whenever her daughter looks at it she will always be reminded of her mom's silly side.

Supplies: Cardstock (Bazzill); patterned paper (Creative Imaginations, Once Upon a Scribble); stamps (Fontwerks, Inkadinkado); stickers (SEI); ribbon (BasicGrey); rub-ons (Heidi Swapp); adhesive (Therm O Web); Misc: ink, pen

Artwork: Erin Derkatz

Use Ephemera

You are bound to find some wonderful things on your search: old stamps and letters, necklaces, books, handwritten love notes and more. These treasures are excellent for including in your albums and on scrapbook pages. Be creative in the ways you include these things. They are definitely an important part of the story, and preserving them will keep them from getting lost or damaged.

Artwork: Michele Skinner

An excellent source to search for ephemera is the local library. If you know that an ancestor or family member was somehow involved in any public group, organization or sports team, you can bet they were covered by their local paper at one point or another. Newspaper articles and photos make great additions to scrapbook pages. Try combining them with photos of your own the way Michelle did here, for added interest and color.

Supplies: Cardstock (Bazzill); patterned paper (My Mind's Eye); letter stickers (American Crafts); embellishments (7gypsies, Me & My Big Ideas, Scenic Route); ribbon (May Arts); adhesive (3M, Tombow)

creative*sparks*

What the heck does ephemera mean anyway? The word ephemera basically means short-lived. Some examples of ephemera include baseball cards, playbills, ticket stubs, letters, postcards, envelopes, stamps, scorecards and anything else of that nature.

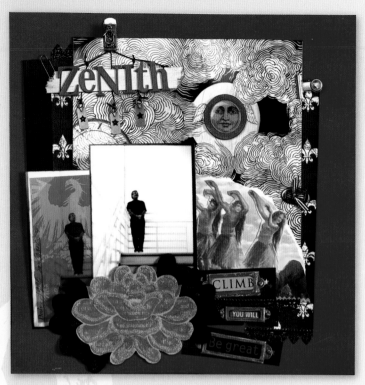

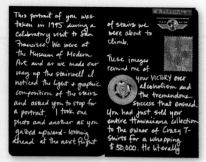

This portrait of you was taken in 1995 during a celebratory visit to San Francisco. We were at the Museum of Modern Art and as we made our way up the stairwell I noticed the light & graphic composition of the stairs and asked you to stop for a portrait. I took one photo and another as you gazed upward - looking ahead at the next flight of stairs we were about to climb.

These images remind me of your VICTORY over alcoholism and the tremendous success that ensued. You had just sold your entire Hawaiiana collection to the owner of Crazy T-Shirts for a whopping $50,000. He literally

Ephemera can add a wonderfully personal touch to your layouts. Here, Cindy went to her father's extensive collection of 1940s Hawaiian antiques. The moon image is a photocopy from a book that she printed onto a transparency and then painted on the back. Using a scanner or photocopier to include copies of ephemera is a great way to keep the original piece intact.

Supplies: Cardstock, flower (Bazzill); patterned paper (Do You Digi, Prima); chipboard letters (Heidi Swapp); chipboard accent (Technique Tuesday); stickers (EK Success, Making Memories); transparencies (Magic Scraps); ribbon (May Arts); bookplates (Junkitz, Making Memories); label, photo turns, rub-on (7gypsies); library pocket (Autumn Leaves); brads, clip (Making Memories); crystals (Swarovski); rhinestones (Prima); Misc: foil trim, glitter, ink, paint, pen, watercolors, wing accents

Artwork: Cindy Ellen Russell

creative *sparks*

If you can't find any good vintage ephemera during your investigation, there are some wonderful places online to find some great authentic ephemera you can substitute. One of my favorite stores is Papier Valise (www.papiervalise.com) based out of Canada. It has some of the most interesting and fun ephemera around. Of course, if you need only a bit of ephemera here and there, you could always check out one of the kit clubs that includes ephemera with their monthly mailings.

This image of my father as a kid playing with model planes reminded me of an old book I had lying around that used to belong to him. After I found the book, I noticed that the copyright was dated around the same time as the photograph. While thumbing through the pages, a thirty-year-old stamp commemorating the first flight of the Wright Brothers dropped out. I decided that the stamp and the book were the perfect ephemera for my page. I used the stamp as inspiration for the color palette and then made photocopies of one of the pages to add a finishing touch.

Supplies: Patterned paper (Bo-Bunny, CherryArte, Rouge de Garance); letter stickers (American Crafts); die cut (CherryArte); rub-on (Hambly); stamps (Sugarloaf); ink (Ranger)

creative *techniques*

Distressing Ephemera

If you're interested in distressing ephemera, using a photocopy is a wonderful way to include it in a scrapbook page without having to tear apart the original piece. Follow these steps to make your photocopy look more interesting and authentic.

Materials

- Book, letter or envelope to copy
- Copy machine
- Scissors or paper trimmer
- Distress ink
- Small cup of water
- Small mister bottle filled with water

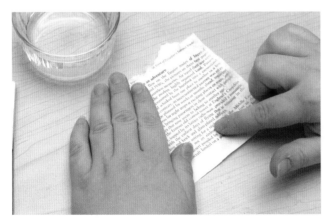

1 Start by making a color copy of your piece. Making a color copy, even if the piece is white paper with black type, will preserve some of the natural aging and distressing marks to give your image more depth. Trim excess paper from your piece, leaving only the image of the original.

2 Crumple up the piece a few times to give it some wear and tear. Add a few strong creases by folding the paper back and forth a few times at one or two of the corners. Tear along the top or bottom edge for added interest.

3 Moisten the tips of your fingers and run them along some of the creases on the page. Crumple the page again.

4 Run the distress pad along the edges and creases of the paper. Spray lightly with water and allow to dry. Repeat with a second color if desired.

Incorporate!

Use these research techniques together to create unique mini albums. Combine groups of facts to determine an album theme, then search through your photos to see what you have that can support your theme. Use the album ideas covered in the first chapter or create a theme of your own.

Your collection of photos, stories and ephemera for an album or project doesn't need to be chronological. It just needs to follow a common theme. If you have stories that don't have accompanying photos, don't let that stop you from scrapping them. Find another photo with the same subjects to use, or create a layout with no photo at all.

Supplies: Patterned paper (A2Z, American Crafts, BasicGrey, Daisy D's, Oscraps, Prima); die cuts (Daisy D's); felt (American Crafts); label (Dymo); ribbon (SEI, Strano); rub-ons (Hambly); stamps (Purple Onion, Sugarloaf); stars, vintage labels and tags (Papier Valise); adhesive (Scrapbook Adhesive by 3L); Misc: brad, ink, pen

Once you begin to gather stories, you'll find that they start to take on a theme of their own. Put them together to tell another, bigger story of what was important in the life of your relative or ancestor.

Tags are a great way to combine a variety of photos and stories that might otherwise seem disjointed. Keep embellishments on tags simple. Feature the photo on one side, and write corresponding journaling or dates on the other side.

When searching through relatives' old possessions, be sure to look over each one thoroughly. Something that doesn't appear to be anything special at first may hold a treasure trove of interesting ephemera. Look in the bindings of Bibles, beneath old drawers and in hidden compartments in jewelry boxes. You never know what you'll find.

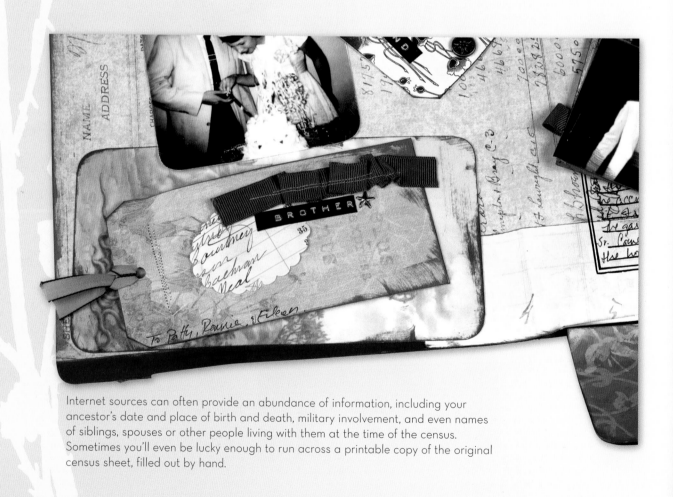

Internet sources can often provide an abundance of information, including your ancestor's date and place of birth and death, military involvement, and even names of siblings, spouses or other people living with them at the time of the census. Sometimes you'll even be lucky enough to run across a printable copy of the original census sheet, filled out by hand.

creative *techniques*

Stitching a Gathered Ribbon

A gathered ribbon can add a soft touch to layouts and other projects. It adds the same variation in texture as a plain straight ribbon, but without the harsh vertical or horizontal line. It can, however, be difficult to keep the ribbon where you'd like it and stitch it with folds intact without stabbing your fingers. This easy technique solves those problems.

Materials
- Ribbon
- Embroidery thread
- Scissors
- Sewing machine
- Embroidery needle
- Tweezers (optional)

1 Trim a piece of ribbon to the desired length. Tie a knot in one end of a piece of embroidery thread and hand baste (stitch loosely) from one end of the ribbon to the other.

2 Hold the end of the embroidery thread in one hand and gather the ribbon along the thread in the other. (Note: You may need to baste two rows of thread in wider ribbons to keep them from curling.) Tie a knot in the end of the thread to hold the gathers.

3 Loosely tack the ribbon onto your project or layout by inserting the needle down through the ribbon and the paper, coming back up close to the original insertion point and knotting the two ends. Repeat this every couple of inches.

4 Use your sewing machine to permanently attach the gathered ribbon to the page.

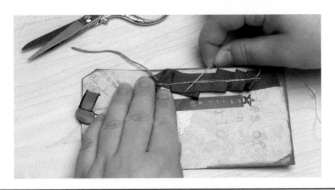

5 Use small scissors to clip the knots in the embroidery thread. Pull all visible embroidery thread to remove it from the ribbon. Use tweezers if you have trouble grasping the thread with your fingers.

meet me

in PaRiS

Bob Sampson decided to go to
Paris for his first weekend of
leave in a long time. While he
was visiting the Louvre, he ran into
two of his best friends. None of them knew
the others had the weekend off, or that they
had planned to visit Paris! Every year after
that, they had their pictures taken in the
same pose, just like that day at the Louvre.

Chapter three

Saying It with Color

Scrapbook artists are so well trained to match layout colors to photo colors that often heritage layouts turn out dull, drab and boring in various shades of brown or gray. Give your ancestors new life by choosing colors that represent who they were. Were they bold and beautiful? Soft and subtle? Or maybe a little bonkers? Color portrays emotion. Tell their story accurately by choosing colors that make it impossible to ignore your family's personality. Just don't forget your own in the process. Your pages are your canvas. This is your work of art. Let down your inhibitions and create what you are inspired to. If you do so, the page will be more moving to everyone who views it, and it will impact your relatives for generations to come.

But don't stop there. Mix and match patterns and textures as well as various embellishments to create a page that truly celebrates your family members for who they were. This chapter will start by covering the basics of color theory and then move on to all kinds of inspirational projects to help you realize new ways of combining color, texture and embellishments for a truly spectacular page.

Use Color Theory

I'm sure you've come across a color wheel before, but it never hurts to have a refresher. A color wheel is an invaluable tool when it comes to choosing colors for a page. Learning the basics of combining colors directly from the wheel will help you with mixing and matching a variety of hues for your everyday pages. Remember when you are choosing colors in various combinations to also vary the value (lightness or darkness) of the color. For example, choosing the complementary colors of a basic green and a basic red won't have nearly as striking of an effect as a dark olive mixed with a soft pink. It takes a bit of practice and patience, but it's well worth the time. Plus, experimenting with color can be loads of fun!

creative *sparks*

There are so many cool ways to create basic color combinations. Pull out your color wheel and refer to this handy guide the next time you are stuck on how to mix and match color.

Complementary: *Two colors directly across from one another. (Example: red and green)*

Triadic: *Three colors equidistant from each other. (Example: green, purple and orange)*

Monochromatic: *One color in varying shades of light and dark. (Example: robin's egg blue, royal blue and navy)*

Analogous: *Three colors directly adjacent to each other. (Example: red, orange and yellow)*

Complementary colors can create a striking effect. On this layout I combined a crimson red with a bright turquoise. Place complementary-colored accents on a neutral background to really make them pop off the page.

Supplies: Cardstock (WorldWin); patterned paper (Hambly, Prima); stamps (Technique Tuesday); adhesive (Therm O Web); Misc: ink

Change the values of color combinations to give them even more depth and interest. On this layout Crystal chose a complementary combination of blue and orange. She went with a lighter shade of blue to make it really stand out against this vibrant orange.

Supplies: Cardstock (WorldWin); patterned paper (American Crafts, Autumn Leaves, KI Memories); letter stickers (American Crafts); rub-ons (American Traditionals); ribbon (Stemma); adhesives (3L); Misc: decorative scissors, pen

The most basic and well-known triadic color scheme (red, yellow and blue) can create stunning results. Here, the darker background allows the white in the photos to really stand out, allowing them to become the main focus of the page.

Supplies: Cardstock (Bazzill); patterned paper (Li'l Davis); ribbon (BasicGrey); printable transparency (Staples); adhesive (EK Success, Elmer's); Misc: paint, pen

creative*sparks*

Add color and dimension to chipboard letters by applying chalk ink directly to the surface. Two or three coats works best, and remember to allow the chipboard to dry fully before placing it anywhere near your work in progress.

Here, Lana took her color scheme to the next level by continuing it into her own handwriting for the quote on the bottom right. The layout is further accentuated by the use of the black-and-white striped ribbon across the bottom third of the layout, which adds contrast for the lime, fuchsia and teal combination to further stand out.

Supplies: Cardstock (Bazzill); patterned paper (Autumn Leaves, Creative Imaginations); chipboard numbers (Fancy Pants); flowers (Making Memories, Petaloo); ribbon (Jo-Ann); rub-ons (Hambly, Melissa Frances); button (Autumn Leaves); adhesive (Aleene's, Tombow); Misc: glitter, paint, pen

Artwork: Lana Rappette

A monochromatic color scheme can often create a striking layout. The black and white patterned paper that Lana used here nicely brings out the contrast in the black-and-white photo. The variation of reds and pinks portrays all of the passion and difficulty of young love that is expressed in her journaling. Choose a color that conveys the mood of your page, then play with different values of light and dark for a striking effect.

Supplies: Cardstock (Die Cuts with a View); buttons, patterned paper, sticker accents (KI Memories); letter stickers (American Crafts, Chatterbox); adhesive (Tombow); Misc: pen

Artwork: Lana Rappette

Artwork: Cindy Ellen Russell

Here, Cindy took cues from the trees in her photo for the color in her layout. The green monochromatic color scheme is composed in way that leads the eye around the page, and when it lands on the color photo, you are instantly drawn in. The color photo against the green monochromatic page makes the photo appear almost as a window into the world of her family legacy.

Supplies: Cardstock (Bazzill); patterned paper (BasicGrey, Frances Meyer); letter stickers (American Crafts, Colorbok, EK Success, Making Memories); brad clip, felt trim (Making Memories); crystal (Swarovski); eyelets (Karen Foster); journaling blocks (Colorbok, Creative Imaginations, Heidi Swapp); label (Paper Source); mask (Heidi Swapp); origami mesh (Aitoh); ribbon (May Arts); stamp (Hero Arts); stickers (EK Success, Hallmark); tag (KI Memories); pin (Paperchase); watercolor pencils (Crayola); Misc: epoxy, ink, pen

creative*sparks*

To reduce bulk on the front of your layout (and subsequent creases in your layout) when adding paper clips to the front of your page, first use a craft knife to make a small slit in your background paper or cardstock. Then slide the back part of the clip through the paper.

Mix and Match Patterns

When it comes to patterned papers, I like to mix things up a bit. After choosing my photo, I skim through my paper collection and grab anything that jumps out at me. Once I'm done, I take a look at what I have. From there I usually select one or two papers and then add to them. My advice is to toss out any of those old adages concerning pattern combinations. It's often pleasing to combine florals with stripes, dots with paisleys or stripes with plaids. You never know what you will come up with. Start by coordinating the colors in the patterned paper, and then let your eye guide you to pleasing pattern combinations. If you're still unsure, simply select papers from the same manufacturer and line to be guaranteed everything will coordinate.

If you are going for a funky, eclectic look but are feeling a bit color-challenged, use papers from the same line. You just need to look a little farther to find the perfect one. For this digital layout, I selected a kit with a wide variety of bright colors. I then enhanced those colors by repeating them in the text. Choose colors from the patterned papers for your title and journaling for a well-coordinated page.

Supplies: Software (Adobe); digital background graphic, patterned paper by Doris Castle (Scrapbook Graphics); paper tears by Steph Krush (Digital Paper Tearing)

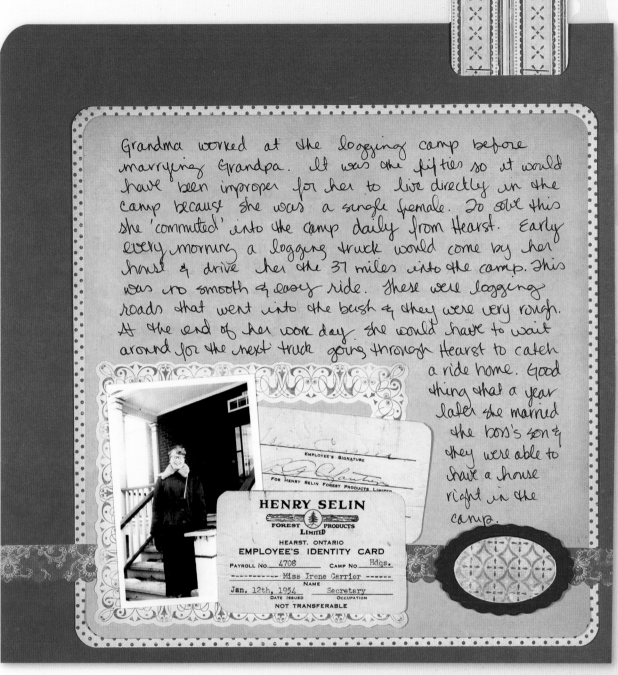

Grandma worked at the logging camp before marrying Grandpa. It was the fifties so it would have been improper for her to live directly in the camp because she was a single female. To solve this she 'commuted' into the camp daily from Hearst. Early every morning a logging truck would come by her house & drive her the 37 miles into the camp. This was no smooth & easy ride. These were logging roads that went into the bush & they were very rough. At the end of her work day she would have to wait around for the next truck going through Hearst to catch a ride home. Good thing that a year later she married the boss's son & they were able to have a house right in the camp.

HENRY SELIN
FOREST PRODUCTS
LIMITED
HEARST, ONTARIO
EMPLOYEE'S IDENTITY CARD
PAYROLL NO. 4708   CAMP NO. Hdqs.
------- Miss Irene Carrier -------
NAME
Jan. 12th, 1954   Secretary
DATE ISSUED   OCCUPATION
NOT TRANSFERABLE

Artwork: Crystal Jeffrey Rieger

Choose a colorful line of papers and mix and match various patterns and colors within that line. This allows you to have a variety of color without the stress of deciding which colors actually match. It's likely that line also offers various embellishments that will nicely round out your page. Throw in a piece of vintage ephemera and you're done!

Supplies: Die-cut embellishments, patterned paper (My Mind's Eye); chipboard (Li'l Davis); adhesive (Scrapbook Adhesive by 3L); Misc: paint, pen

Lee

High school graduation, 1967 - On my way to college with dreams and plans of becoming a doctor. Funny how life has a way of changing the best laid plans. Forty years later, 2 children, 4 grandchildren, and working to help support children. Rewards of another kind!

Choose patterns by coordinating with one or two of the accent colors in your main background paper. Here, I started with the pink abstract floral paper, added the green paper for contrast and finished with the dot pattern. The turquoise blue in the dots brings out the touches of blue in the background paper and also coordinates nicely with the green. Select a patterned paper you really like, then add more patterns with one or two of the colors from your original paper. Slowly build on the combination, adding and taking away papers as necessary, until you have a result you are pleased with.

Supplies: Software (Adobe); patterned paper by Ronee Parsons (Oscraps) and Sausan Designs (Scrapbook Graphics); frame, label, ribbon by Vicki Stegall (Oscraps)

Artwork: Catherine Feegel-Erhardt

Another way to combine patterns and add color is to begin with a geometric background paper. Here, Catherine used a grid pattern and stamped over it with circular shapes in contrasting colors. Another fun idea is to apply colored rub-ons or more intricate stamp designs. You'll find that once you master this technique, it is a quick and easy way to add depth and dimension to a layout.

Supplies: Cardstock (Bazzill); patterned paper (Hambly); ribbon (American Crafts); reinforcement labels (Avery); adhesive (Aleene's, EK Success); Misc: ink, paint

creative*sparks*

Try stamping with items other than stamps. In the layout above, Catherine used a child's plastic cup to stamp the large circles and the end of an empty toilet paper roll to stamp the small circles. There are endless household items that can be turned into scrapbooking tools with a little bit of ink or paint and some creativity. Don't let yourself be fooled into thinking that you can only use items made specifically for scrapbooking.

Use Embellishments to Add Color

Embellishments are perfect for adding bursts of color. The perfect flower, tag or letter can take a page from simple to stunning. Use embellishments in accent colors to add dimension to your page. Or use embellishments of an entirely different color to draw attention toward a specific part of the page.

Brighten up old, colorless photos by customizing your embellishments to match your page. Here, I wanted to bring out the color of the circular transparency overlay in the background so I custom-colored the letters and the metal clips at the bottom of the page in varying shades of green to create depth. Give the main colors of your layout an extra boost by adding a splash of a complementary color to your title.

Supplies: Cardstock (WorldWin); transparency (Hambly); letter stickers (BasicGrey, KI memories); mask, transparent letters (Heidi Swapp); sticker (Stemma); found objects (Papier Valise); adhesive (Scrapbook Adhesive by 3L, Therm O Web); ink (Ranger)

Creating Custom-colored Letters

Alcohol inks are great for adding color to letters. They are easy to use, and it's always fun to see what different color combinations you can create.

Materials

- 2–3 colors of alcohol ink
- Acetate letters or other items to color
- Alcohol ink applicator
- Newsprint or scrap paper

1 Cover your work area with newsprint or scrap paper and arrange the letters you would like to color. If desired, wear gloves to avoid staining your fingers. Place a felt pad onto the alcohol ink applicator. Apply two or three colors of ink directly to the pad.

2 Stamp the applicator directly onto each of the letters. For a vibrant effect, stamp and pull the applicator directly up. For a more subtle effect, softly swipe the applicator across the letters.

Strategically placed embellishments and letters in contrasting colors are a great way to add visual interest to your page. For this layout, I used a deep crimson-red patterned paper as the main background and added the light green flowers and letters to give the layout more depth. Choose an accent color in a complementary shade (directly across on the color wheel) or combine a bright color with a neutral one for maximum effect.

Supplies: Patterned paper (American Crafts, Prima); letter stickers (American Crafts); chipboard (Fancy Pants); brads (SEI); flowers (Prima); adhesive (Scrapbook Adhesive by 3L, Aleene's, Therm O Web)

On this layout, Catherine used a custom-colored cloth diaper pin to coordinate with the owl image at the top. Look for items around the house that you can easily alter. Use paints, alcohol inks, patterned papers and photo transfer techniques to customize these items to boost the colors already on your page.

Supplies: Cardstock (Bazzill); patterned paper (Scenic Route); chipboard letters (Heidi Swapp); rhinestones (EK Success); rub-ons (US Stamp); transparencies (Hambly); adhesive (EK Success, Plaid); glossy topcoat (Ranger); Misc: ink, paint

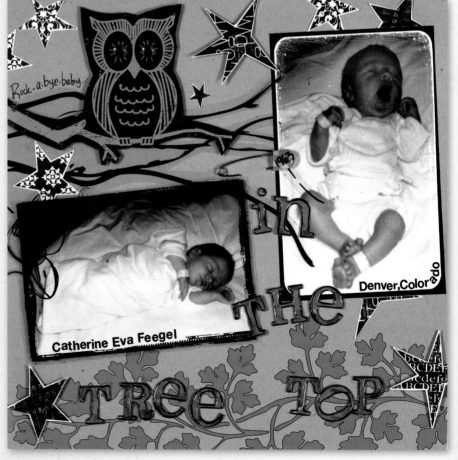

Artwork: Catherine Feegel-Erhardt

scrapbooking is stupid

That's what they say, those people who thumb their noses at this hobby and say it's a flash in the pan, or a pasttime for fat moms with money to burn and time to kill. But the point "they" are missing is this: if no one scrapbooked - and disregard the notion of ribbons, stickers and pretty papers - there would be no history. If no one in my family kept a record, I wouldn't have these photos of my great-grandparents and great uncle playing in the water. Who knew people back then played? Who knew they were just like us? Who would have known who they were if somewhere along the line someone just threw the photos in a box and walked away? I would love to have the memory of this day in their words but I don't. But luckily, my kids will have memories from their days because I DO write it down. I am keeping their history alive. And that isn't stupid.

Artwork: Michele Skinner

Add brightly colored embellishments to a neutral background to really bring attention to a specific area of your page. On this page, Michele uses the bright red arrow tags to draw the eye to each individual photograph. This helps bring attention to photographs that may otherwise blend into the background page.

Supplies: Cardstock (It Takes Two); number stickers, photo turns (7gypsies); border sticker (My Mind's Eye); clear pebble (Making Memories); adhesive (3M, Tombow); Misc: brads

Use a white background to make colors jump off your page. The clean slate provided by a white background gives you the freedom to add embellishments, letters and doodles in any combination of colors. On this layout, I started with a teal label and combined it with a yellow photo turn. From there, the rest of the color combination came together. On a layout like this, make sure to use each color in two different places so that no one color is out of place.

Supplies: Software (Adobe); digital flowers, label, letters, overlays by Vicki Stegall (Oscraps); flower doodle by Ida (Catscrap); photo turn by Laura Alpuche (Oscraps); puff stickers by Sausan Designs (Scrapbook Graphics)

Follow Your Gut!

Sometimes basic color combinations don't give you quite the personality you are trying to express. When choosing a color combination for an entire album, start with a couple of basic colors and expand on them to supply lots of variety throughout the book. Don't forget, if you have a paper with a pattern you like, you can always customize it to fit within your color scheme. You never have to sacrifice color to use a paper or element you like.

Once I chose the basic color combination for the album, I couldn't find a patterned paper appropriate for the cover. I wanted something subtle so the title and handwriting transfer could take center stage, and I wanted the cover to have a peaceful feel, but I also wanted something colorful. I used ink and a stipple brush to create a pattern on plain white cardstock. Never assume that you have to use a pre-made background; step out of your comfort zone to create your own unique creations.

Supplies: Cardstock (WorldWin); patterned paper (Bo-Bunny); letter stickers (American Crafts); chipboard arrow (Everlasting Keepsakes); ribbon (Prima); flowers (Blueye Dezines); adhesive (3M, Scrapbook Adhesive by 3L); ink (Ranger); Misc: colored pencils

creative*sparks*

Once you master using a stipple brush, try stippling through stencils or doodling templates for a subtle background pattern. On the cover of this album featured above, I stippled the outside edges as described in the step-by-step instructions on page 57. I then used a template to create the arrow, which adds a burst of color to the solid white background.

creative *techniques*

Using Ink to Add Color

Ink doesn't have to be reserved for distressing. You can just as easily put your favorite distressing techniques to use as a way to add or enhance color. Instead of reaching for black or brown the next time you want to add some dimension, try grabbing a candy-apple red or a turquoise blue. A whole range of colors is available in a variety of inks. Just remember that a dye-based ink will dry almost immediately when applied to paper, whereas a pigment ink will take a bit longer to dry and has the ability to smudge and smear. Both will work for this technique, depending on how messy or clean you would like your finished project to look.

Materials

- Stipple brush
- Colored ink pad
- Scrap paper
- Background paper or photo mat to ink

1   Cover your work area with scrap paper. Place the background paper you would like to add color to in the center.

2   Dab the stipple brush straight down onto the ink pad until you get a good amount loaded onto the brush.

3   Begin tapping the brush at the edge of your paper with a light circular motion, moving slowly inward. Re-ink your brush as needed. The edges will slowly become darker with ink, leaving a lighter area in the center. It may take some time to get used to the amount of ink and pressure to use, but once you do, you'll find many ways of applying this technique.

When choosing colors for your albums, find an image or piece of ephemera for inspiration and then take it to the next level. In this photo, I loved the soft pinks and blues combined with the weathered browns of the old wood because they elicit such a serene feeling. I decided to use those colors as inspiration, but I wanted something a little bit funkier. I chose a blue just a bit darker, and then took the pink up a notch to this fun fuchsia color. Once you've found your inspiration and chosen a few basic colors, expand on them to create a variegated palette for your entire album.

Supplies: Cardstock (WorldWin); patterned paper (American Crafts, Dove of the East, Hambly, Stemma); transparency (Hambly); letter stickers (American Crafts, SEI); letter stamps (Sugarloaf); stamp (Purple Onion); flower (Blueye Dezines); ribbon, tag (Stemma); rub-ons (Imaginisce); adhesive (Scrapbook Adhesives by 3L, Therm O Web); Misc: brad, colored pencils, ink

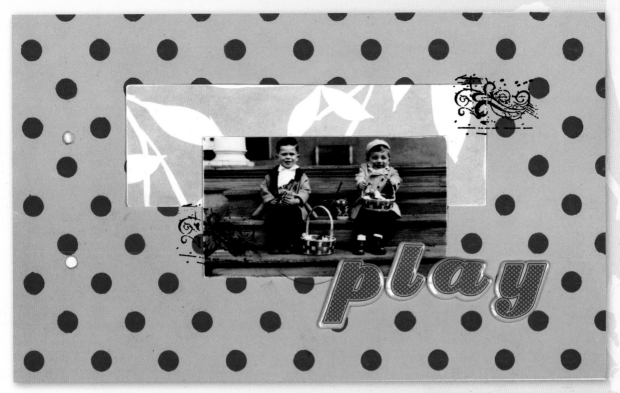

You can always easily customize a patterned paper with paint, ink or colored pencils. Don't sacrifice using a great patterned paper just because the color is off. The background paper for this page originally had orange dots. While the orange would look great on this page, it doesn't quite blend with the rest of the album. For an easy fix, I used a colored pencil to recolor them. It gave the page a young feel that tied in the cute faces in the photo.

Just because you've chosen a color scheme for your album doesn't mean you can't mix it up a bit. I wanted to add something different and fun to make this page stand out more. The photo is so small that it left the page feeling rather empty. I added the green flower to give it a whole new dimension. Every now and then, try something unexpected to add an extra special touch to your page.

Accent soft colors on a page by coloring a doodle or stamped image with coordinating, but brighter, colored pencils. Here, the page needed just a little something extra. I had used arrows elsewhere in the album, and decided to add a hand-drawn arrow for a little punch of color. The result takes the page from calm and quiet to fun and funky.

creative *techniques*

Using Colored Pencils

Colored pencils are definitely an overlooked item when it comes to scrapbooking. They are so quick and easy to pull out; you'd have to be crazy not to carry them with you for use at a moment's notice. Use colored pencils the next time you have a patterned paper that's just not quite right, or to create a pattern completely from scratch on white cardstock. They are an excellent resource when it comes to customizing colors to get just the right effect.

Materials

- Colored pencils
- Drawn or stamped image
- Mineral spirits (available at art and stamp stores)
- Blending stump
- Sandpaper

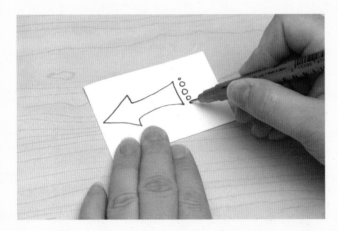

1 Draw or stamp the design or title you wish to color. If you are stamping and would prefer that the original outline not show, use an embossing ink. This will allow you to see only a light outline of the stamp or design that will not be noticeable once the color is added.

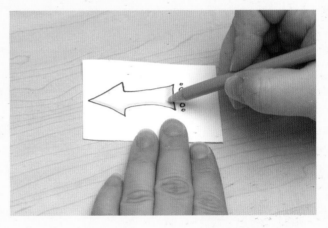

2 Add a thick line of color around the outside edges of your original image.

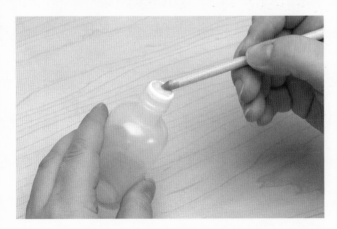

3 Soak the tip of the blending stump in mineral spirits. The mineral spirits will break down the lead of the colored pencil and wash the color into the center leaving a watercolor effect. Practice with different amounts of color and blending to get the desired result.

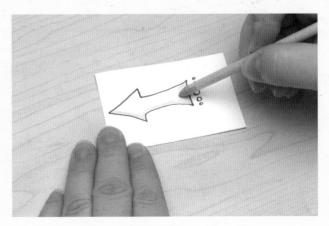

4 Use the tip to blend the color toward the center of the image.

cedar
street

The Myers kids lived in a huge house on Cedar Street in Spokane. Grandma worked while Grandpa went to school.

Looking Your Best

You've done the research, dug up stories, spoken to relatives and chosen a color palette. But what if the photo you want to use on your layout is looking less than spectacular? In this chapter, you'll discover a few basic tricks you can use to clean up a photo using digital tools you probably already have in your arsenal (i.e., a scanner, a computer and software programs such as Photoshop Elements, Photoshop Creative Suite II and ACDSee). If you don't have these items at your disposal, or if you have photos that are beyond digital repair, turn the pages to find some other techniques for enhancing photos the old-fashioned way. On most pages, the photo is the focal point, so you always want it looking its best.

Scan Your Photos

Scanning photos is so much better than using the original hard copies for a number of reasons. First and foremost, it saves the original to be scanned and used again in another layout or album. (I am all about scrapping a great photo two or three times!) Second, it allows you to make basic changes and conversions, such as transforming a color photo to a black and white. And third, it allows you to make adjustments in your digital program so that the photo looks just a tad bit better than it did before.

Walter and Maxie Simmons had the love of a lifetime. Walter made Maxie's gorgeous wedding clothing by hand. This photo was taken on that day in Olympia, Washington in 1916.

love of a lifetime

Some photos will be so well preserved that you won't need to make any changes after scanning. The photo in this layout is a copy of a copy, and it still came out looking wonderful. If the original photo is still looking brilliant, you can generally scan it and print a copy in the same size that will come out looking just as great.

Supplies: Software (Adobe); digital cardstock (Shabby Shoppe); paper tears by Steph Krush (Digital Paper Tearing); patterned paper by Sausan Designs (Scrapbook Graphics) and Ronee Parsons (Oscraps)

Shelton

Using a heavily distressed background paper allows the bright white of this vintage photo to look crisp and clean. When you're lucky enough to find a photo that you can scan and use as is, choose colors and patterns that allow the photo to become the focus of the page.

Supplies: Digital patterned paper by Jackie Eckles (Little Dreamer); brush, stitching accents (Sausan Designs); labels (Windgefleuster Designs); rubber bands by Vicki Stegall (Oscraps)

creative *sparks*

Here are a few tips to keep in mind when using a scanner.

*Before scanning your photos, wipe the photo and scanner clean with a dry, lint-free cloth.

*Scan photos at 300 dpi or higher.

*Scan all photos as a color photo regardless of whether the original is color or black and white.

(This allows you to have the most control over any digital adjustments you'll make later.)

Restore Worn Photos

Many heritage photos are cracked, creased and dusty. There's no getting around that. There are, however, a few simple ways to restore them with just a little bit of knowledge about your computer and image-editing software.

The Clone Stamp tool allows you to replace color one pixel at a time in damaged areas of a photo. This tool will allow you to choose a place on the photo from which it will sample the replacement color for the damaged area. The Clone Stamp tool works best for fixing small scratches and spots.

This photo has some slight spots of discoloration and scratches.

With the Clone Stamp, I'm able to replace those discolorations with other parts of the photo that are undamaged. Then I am free to create a layout that isn't distracted by the damaged photo and still focuses on my grandfather's face.

Supplies: Software (Adobe); digital background paper by Ronee Parsons (Oscraps); transparency by Sausan Designs (Scrapbook Graphics); letter stamps by Michelle Coleman (ScrapArtist); envelope tie, label, overlay, petals, staple by Vicki Stegall (Oscraps); frame by Lie Fhung (Ztampf); photo corner by Melgen Designs (Oscraps); tags by Maya (Scrapbook Graphics) and Melgen Designs (Oscraps)

This photo has many flaws. The most noticeable are the stains on the upper right, some of them extending on to the main subjects.

You can see that with the stains removed, the focus of the photo is directed back to the subjects. Cindy used the Clone Stamp to re-color the stained areas to match the clear areas of the photo. The result is a striking photograph with good contrast. Cindy also used brightly contrasting colors in her composition to enhance the newly repaired black-and-white contrast of the photo.

Supplies: Patterned paper (Chronicle Books, Scenic Route); letter stickers, sticker accents (EK Success); bottle cap (Li'l Davis); chipboard letters (American Crafts); paper trim (Doodlebug); rub-ons (Daisy D's, Li'l Davis); stamps (Hero Arts, Sassafras Lass, Plaid); Misc: colored pencils, ink, pens, watercolors

Artwork: Cindy Ellen Russell

creative*sparks*

Using a folder as your background like Cindy did in the layout above adds another dimension to your scrapping by giving you the interior of the folder to decorate or fill.

Utilize the Patch Tool

The Patch tool allows you to essentially cut out a piece of the photo and replace it with a "patch" from another area of the photo. This tool works well for replacing stains in the background of the photo.

The Patch tool is an excellent choice for cleaning up the stain in the lower right corner of this photo.

The Patch tool allows me to move the grass from an undamaged area and place it directly over the stain. The program automatically blends the patch into its new surroundings giving it a seamless repair.

Supplies: Cardstock (WorldWin); patterned paper (American Crafts); letter stickers (SEI); flowers (Prima); stamps (Gel-a-tins); adhesive (3L); Misc: ink

This photo is completely torn in half! The line across the center is an actual tear.

With a little bit of patience the Patch tool can work miracles. It's nearly impossible to tell that this photo had been torn. By carefully arranging the two pieces next to each other before scanning, and spending a few minutes using the Patch tool, Crystal completely restored this photo to brand new.

Supplies: Cardstock (WorldWin); transparency (Hambly); patterned paper (Polar Bear Press); ribbon (Michaels); label (Papier Valise); adhesive (Scrapbook Adhesives by 3L); Misc: pens

every family has a colorful past...

This might or might not be the original great grandma selin. we don't know 'cause she was placed in a mental home & never spoken of again.

Artwork: Crystal Jeffrey Rieger

Enhance Photos with the Curves Tool

The word "curves" in relation to photos and image-editing software refers to the adjustment of the contrast in a photo. In your image-editing program, the Curves tool is a diagonal line that represents all the colors in the photo. By moving different parts of the line, you can make the light parts lighter and the dark parts darker. This can give a much-needed boost to photos that have lost contrast with aging. Reference a manual or use the "Help" feature in your image-editing program to learn specifics on how to use the Curves tool.

You can see how the colors in this photo have begun to acquire a similar intensity over time. The Curves tool can work wonders on photos like this one by adding back in the contrast between dark and light.

Here you can see how the Curves tool made the dark colors dark and the light colors light. Further accentuate this contrast by using a light background color with darker accents and embellishments.

Supplies: Cardstock (WorldWin); patterned paper (SEI); letter stickers (American Crafts); chipboard (Fancy Pants); adhesive (3L); Misc: pen

The details in this photo have become washed out, and the contrast has faded over time.

By adjusting the curves, the small details like the wire fence, the folds in the subject's jacket and the lines in his face become more noticeable. This gives the photo extra power and strength. Use the Curves tool on worn photos when you would like to bring back the details of the original image.

Supplies: Software (Adobe); digital background, brad, pen by Maya (Scrapbook Graphics); flowers, leaves by Sausan Designs (Scrapbook Graphics); lace by Stacey Jewell Stahl (Digital Scrapbook Artisan Guild); splatters by Meryl Bartha (Digital Scrapbook Place)

Robert Berry,
I look at you, a man I never met, and I'm connected, and back. I wonder why you did marry, you certainly must had lots of women noticing you. My friends and I still think you look like a movie star. My son Jeremy reminds me very much of you, only small now. I wonder if he will grow up to look even more like you? I can't tell if he'll have your strong body yet or whether he'll be the amazing athlete you were. He's got that manliness, determination, affection and that love of family that comes through in so many of you photos. I can only imagine what your death in your 30's cost you family. You, the firstborn, gone At least know you are still remembered, that your presence is felt today.

Artwork: Karen Bowers

Learn to Use Filters and Actions

Filters and actions are quick and easy fixes for photos that need just a slight tune-up. They are easy to use, and with just a little research into your image-editing program, you'll be able to find a few that work well for you.

This beautiful wedding-day photo has a lot of distracting scratches and dust.

Katrina used the Dust and Scratches filter in Photoshop to quickly and easily clean up this photo. You can see what an improvement such a small step can make. Look in the "Help" section or search online for tutorials for using filters or actions in your specific program that can achieve similar results.

Supplies: Cardstock (Bazzill); brads, patterned paper, ribbon, rub-ons (One Heart One Mind); stamp (Autumn Leaves); adhesive (Duck); Misc: ink

Artwork: Katrina Simeck

72

The colors in this photo are a little gray. Although the subject of the photo is great, it just doesn't have the "wow" factor. Use filters to enhance the mood in photos like this one.

WISHING YOU COULD KNOW THIS NOW

LITTLE ME

nothing scary lived in our house in Rhode Island. there were no lobsters in the toilet. Tell mom about that kid who tried to strangle you. Go out for track in junior high school. Do not date Alex or Michael. Take more English Literature classes in college. At the college art show, find the artist who made that brass sculpture and buy it. Go to Washington DC after college. Trust the vibes you get from people. know that God really is trustworthy even with mysteries. Read His book more. you will be the artist you long to be, but you will have to wait a long time. you are a good writer, but sadly the great works of poetry you wrote in high school are just dreck. Darn. Go to a doctor in the 1st year of trying to conceive. accepting the label of infertile for awhile will bring you children sooner. When Grandpas boxes get shipped out here, make sure Frank counts the boxes and that none are missing. mom will survive cancer many times. Imagine having sons not daughters!

circa 1968

Artwork: Karen Bowers

By applying a radiant filter provided by Virtual Photographer, a free download at Optik Verve Labs, and changing the blend modes of the layers, Karen is able to make the colors in the photo really pop. The photo takes on a whimsical and dreamy effect perfect for her layout.

Supplies: Software (Adobe); digital label, patterned paper by Doris Castle (Scrapbook Graphics); flowers (Digital Scrapbook Artisan Guild, Scrapbook Graphics); frame by Ronee Parsons (Oscraps); glass pebble (Digital Scrapbook Artisan Guild)

This photo has become washed out with age. The once vibrant colors are dull, and the photo has started to yellow.

Artwork: Cindy Ellen Russell

Here Cindy chose to use a filter to give the photo the appearance of being taken with a pin-hole camera. The filter she used creates a vignette around the photo, bringing the focus back to the main subject. This photo action also removes some of the yellow discoloration and increases the saturation, bringing back some of the color in the flowers.

Supplies: Cardstock (Bazzill); patterned paper (SEI); button, letter stickers (Doodlebug); arrow (Heidi Swapp); brads (Making Memories, SEI); chipboard (Fancy Pants, Li'l Davis, Maya Road, Pressed Petals); clips, photo turns (Making Memories); corrective tape (3M); title mask (Pressed Petals); highlighter tape (Lee Products); label, sticker accents (Autumn Leaves); flowers, photo corners (American Crafts); photo corners, reinforcement stickers (Creative Imaginations); rhinestones (Darice); photo action by Valerie Foster (Do You Digi?); Misc: colored pencils, paint, pen

This photo is pretty good at first glance, but there are a few knicks and scratches.

Using a free downloadable filter program from Polaroid, I was able to easily clean up most of the knicks and scratches in this photo. Without the filter program, fixing scratches like these could have taken hours. But with just a few clicks I have a nice clean image to scrap.

Supplies: Digital letter tabs, overlay by Vicki Stegall (Oscraps); doodle, flower (Sausan Designs)

creative*sparks*

Many online digital scrapbooking shops also offer awesome actions for use in a variety of programs. These actions can take a photo from worn and plain to spectacular with just the touch of a button.

Find Creative Solutions

What? You aren't a computer guru? That's OK. Many heritage photos may be beyond repair for anyone less than a professional. Don't let this stop you from scrapping them. There are a lot of ways to distract viewers from the imperfections in your photos and focus their attention on your main subject and journaling. It just takes a bit of creativity, which you have plenty of!

Extraction is an effective way to bring the subject of your photo to center stage and get rid of the damaged parts of the photo altogether. In this photo my great-grandmother looked absolutely gorgeous standing so proudly next to her Ford. But for some reason there was a child's foot extending awkwardly from behind her (probably my mischievous grandfather hiding from the camera) and the rest of the background was just sort of gray and empty. By carefully cutting around the main subject of the photo, I was able to eliminate those distractions entirely.

Here, I used a photo transfer to capture the mood of the photo without worrying about whether the photo was perfect. A photo transfer is meant to add texture and dimension, and the cracks and creases in a vintage photo will add to that.

Supplies: Album (Maya Road); cardstock (WorldWin); patterned paper (BasicGrey, Hambly, Prima, Urban Lily); felt trim (Queen & Co.); chipboard (Fancy Pants); stamps (Purple Onion); adhesive (3M, Scrapbook Adhesives by 3L); ink (Ranger); Misc: pen

creative *techniques*

Transferring Prints

If you like the mood portrayed in a photograph, but the print itself is not strong enough to hold a page on its own, try using a photo transfer technique. There are many methods for creating photo transfers, but the easiest—and least messy—is a packing tape transfer.

Materials

- Copy machine
- Photograph
- Packing tape
- Scissors
- Bowl
- Water

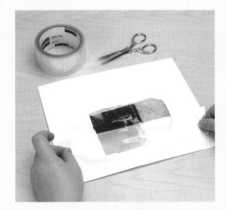

1 Make a photocopy of your image. (Note: printing from an ink-jet printer will not achieve the same result.) Place packing tape in strips across the photocopy until the image is completely covered. Allow for extra lines and wrinkles for added interest, if desired.

2 Burnish (rub hard) the tape with a bone folder or the back of a spoon to remove any air bubbles.

3 Trim the excess paper from the sides of the taped image.

4 Soak the image in a bowl of warm water for 10 to 15 minutes. The more saturated it is, the easier the paper will be to remove.

5 Remove the image from the bowl of water and gently rub the excess paper from the back with your fingers. Rinse the image periodically to remove any stubborn paper lint.

6 Allow the tape to dry, then place it on your cardstock or patterned paper to be added to your layout.

Sometimes a small discoloration can be a positive feature instead of a negative one. Here, I've used a circle to draw attention to the face of one of my photo subjects.

When it seems there is no other choice, you always have the option of distressing a photo even more. Further distressing a photo with sandpaper and ink will bring out the charm in its imperfections.

creative*sparks*

Distressing techniques shouldn't be limited to photos. Try the technique on page 79
with your favorite piece of patterned paper and an interesting chipboard shape to cre-
ate a custom element for your next page.

creative *techniques*

Distressing Photos on Chipboard

With a little elbow grease this technique will give your photos a uniquely distressed look. They will appear as if their edges have been worn down and discolored over time, giving your page tons of charm.

Materials

- Chipboard
- Dry adhesive runner
- Photo to distress
- Ink pad (mix up the colors to change the final look)
- Medium grit sandpaper

1 Scan the original photo. If the original was torn in any way, tear those pieces off the scanned photo print to maintain an authentic feel.

2 Adhere your photo to a piece of chipboard with a strong dry adhesive, and rub a generous amount of ink along the photo where the photo meets the chipboard edges.

3 Use your sandpaper to sand the image of the photo until the white core of the photo paper reveals the outline of your chipboard.

4 Tear the photo along the revealed outline, pulling the free edges toward you (so that the torn edge is left next to the photo). Clean the edges up with sandpaper as desired.

5 Continue alternating sanding and inking the edges of the photo until you achieve the desired look. Then moisten your fingertips and run them along all of the torn edges, slightly rolling them in your fingers. This will finish off the appearance of the distressed photo.

Accent Strong Photos

If you have a really wonderful photo, don't be afraid to draw attention to it. There are many ways to make a strong photo the focal point of a page. Use a different framing style, surround it with smaller supporting photos, place it next to an embellishment in a bold accent color or just plain make it big. Take a look at how some other artists have chosen to accent a few stellar photos that really shine.

When you have a gorgeous photo, take the time to present it properly. This photo was taken by my grandfather while stationed overseas. I have many of his images, but this is the one I always favored while growing up. It's been hanging on my wall for years. I chose to create a simple three-dimensional frame to give the photo the proper display it deserved.

Supplies: Cardstock; patterned paper (Hambly); acrylic letters (Heidi Swapp); rub-on (My Mind's Eye); Misc: brads, dimensional paint, fabric, ink, letter stamps, sticker accents, transparency, twine

creative sparks

To add drama to your page and draw attention to your new frame, consider adding rub-ons or stickers to the transparency.

Making a Simple Shadowbox Frame

Showcase your favorite photos by creating a simple three-dimensional frame with transparencies. The frame mimics the look of a professionally framed photo with glass, giving the display a formal feeling.

Materials

- Paper trimmer
- Craft knife
- Ruler and pencil
- 2 pieces of heavy cardstock in contrasting colors
- Transparencies
- Adhesive
- Dimensional adhesive

1 Trim a rectangle from cardstock to be the same size as your photo. Trim a second piece of cardstock (in a different color) into a rectangle ¼" (6.4mm) smaller than the photo. Apply dry adhesive to the edges to adhere the smaller piece on top of the larger piece.

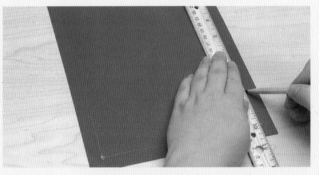

2 Turn the adhered pieces of cardstock over, then measure and mark ½" (1cm) in from each side of the rectangle. Connect the points to create a small rectangle in the center of your piece.

3 Use a craft knife to cut the center from your piece of cardstock following the guides you've drawn.

4 Trim a piece of transparency to the same size as your photo. Adhere the transparency to the back side of the frame with your dry adhesive. Place dimensional adhesive at each corner of the frame along the edges if necessary.

5 Adhere your photo to your layout, then place the completed frame around it.

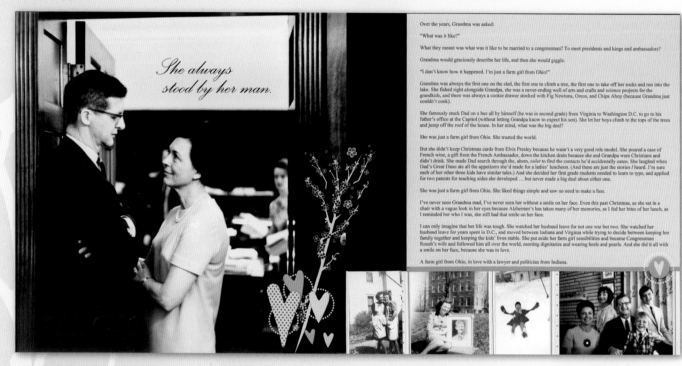

Artwork: Michele Skinner

If you have a group of photos, choose your favorite and enlarge it to take up a good portion of a page. Position the smaller supporting photos around it in a way that allows the reader to glance at them but still lets the large photo take center stage. Here, Michele has enlarged the photo of her grandparents enough to allow it to cover almost the entire left page. The size, combined with the simple title written directly on the photo, draws the eye to this image first.

Supplies: Cardstock (Bazzill); patterned paper (Paper Salon); chipboard hearts (Heidi Grace); rub-ons (7gypsies, American Crafts); adhesive (3M, Tombow)

Artwork: Catherine Feegel-Erhardt

Another way to allow your amazing photo to take center stage is to place it there, literally. By placing your photo in the center of the page and strategically arranging all other elements around it, you can be certain that the viewer of your page will catch all of the exciting details of the picture. If you are really feeling bold, draw the viewer's eye directly into the photo by adding a colorful rub-on directly into the action or scene of the photo.

Supplies: Cardstock (Bazzill); transparencies (Hambly); rub-ons (Hambly, US Stamp); adhesive (Duncan, EK Success, Ranger); Misc: adhesive foam, buttons, floss

Composing a Great Page

There is something about scrapping heritage photos that makes us all revert back to boring. I think part of the reason, for me, is the fact that I may never have known the person I am scrapping about. His or her personality isn't right there to inspire me. But I have found a solution. Once you clean up or digitally alter your photos and have fresh, new copies printed out, spread them out in front of you and take some time to simply stare at them. Shuffle through them one by one and wait until something grabs you. Then observe. Just because your relative isn't sitting right there with you doesn't mean you can't speak to him or her. (Yes, I'm being serious here.) Take a good long look at the photo and ask whatever questions come to mind. Find the answers in the creases around your great-grandfather's eyes, the way your distant aunt folded her hands ever so perfectly in her lap, the loving arm your father threw around his younger brother when they were kids. These are the things that will inspire you. From there, it is only a matter of letting your creative juices flow.

As we discuss unique ways to compose heritage pages and overcome a few of the challenges that heritage photos present, keep in mind the mood of the photo and the clues that the picture gives about your relatives and family as a whole. These are the driving force behind your page, and if you pay attention to them, you can't go wrong.

Scrap Odd-Sized Photos

One major challenge with heritage photos is that many of them are not printed in sizes we are used to. It doesn't seem like that big of a deal when you are working with the photos themselves, but if you are used to dealing with 4" x 6" (10cm x 15cm) photos and are suddenly challenged to work with 5½" x 5½" (14cm x 14cm) images or photos that were once cut into an unusual shape to fit a frame, you will see the difference is extensive. When composing a page with irregular photo sizes you'll find that your design may need to be balanced a bit differently. Try these suggestions for balancing irregular photos on your page in an eye-pleasing way.

Try extending the shape of square photos by adding a rectangular mat that extends further out on one side, or adding a simple strip of patterned paper to extend the shape of the photo. Here, I've added a 2" (5cm) wide strip to the top of this 5" x 5" (13cm x 13cm) photo to create a standard 5" x 7" (13cm x 18cm) shape to design the rest of my page around.

Supplies: Cardstock (WorldWin); patterned paper (American Crafts, SEI); letter stickers (Adornit); rub-ons (Daisy D's); adhesive (Therm O Web); ink (Ranger); Misc: pen

I'm sure she's LAUGHING On the Inside

Modesty masked with mockery. Mom has never really liked her photo taken. Her signature "in your face" look: The Tongue. It reflects that she *is* a goof and it has made for some adorable photos.

Artwork: Lana Rappette

Another way to balance odd-sized photos is to repeat the shape of the photo or photos throughout the layout. This gives the composition a deliberate feel, rather than the feeling that the photo is misshaped or misplaced. Here, Lana had two small square photos and one small rectangular action shot. She repeated the square shape by matting the square background as well as adding a subtle stitch, and then tied in the rectangular shape with a small tag and the position of her journaling. Use this type of repetition to create a pleasing visual design every time.

Supplies: Cardstock (Bazzill); patterned paper (Autumn Leaves, Sweetwater); rub-ons (Autumn Leaves, K&Co.); buttons (Autumn Leaves); flower (American Crafts); tags (SEI)

Shape Up!

A great way to mix up your page composition when scrapping odd-sized photos is to crop them into a circle or another unique shape. When having photos printed, always get extra copies so that you have the opportunity to play around and see what shape you like best.

This was such a sweet photo of my two uncles as toddlers; I just had to scrap it. The problem was that the original photo was a small square that didn't fit well with my other elements. When you have an odd-sized photo, consider cropping it into a shape and incorporating that shape in multiple places throughout your layout. On this layout I cropped the photo into a circle and then created a double mat with patterned paper trimmed to the same shape. Try using this approach with hearts, stars, ovals or any other shape that strikes your fancy.

Supplies: Software (Adobe); digital butterflies, patterned paper by Sausan Designs (Scrapbook Graphics); edge papers, tag by Catrine (Catscrap); number stamp by Michelle Coleman (ScrapArtist)

to sit
and PONDER
the
INTRICACIES
of

*life

I loved the expression on the main subject in this photo, but the original had faded edges and a couple of strange distractions in the background. By cropping the photo into a vertical ellipse I was able to frame the main subject of the photo and bring out a little bit more of that fairytale feeling by eliminating the random distractions in the original photo.

Supplies: Digital cardstock (Shabby Shoppe); patterned paper (Sausan Designs); letter and staple by Vicki Stegall (Oscraps)

Make a Long Story Short

Sometimes you'll find you've collected many stories that have few or no photos to accompany them. There are many ways to include longer journaling entries onto a page, including using hidden journaling techniques, extending the story onto two pages and using the journaling as a design element itself.

TITLE

Here is a basic sketch for including a large amount of journaling. If you don't have a photo, you can use the photo area for ephemera, or even take a current photo of a building or place mentioned in your journaling.

Daniel Howe on my Grandfather; "As I write this, I close my eyes and see the look of

supreme happiness

on the face of this man, in his black beret and khaki shirt, who, in 1979,

traversed the Appalachian Trail with three companions less than half his

age. He had emerged from surgery on his

carotid artery just a few weeks before our reunion hike. At age 79, Nick Gelesko became my hero, again." Appalachian Trail News July 2000

EXPLORE ADVENTURE

Artwork: Lana Rappette

Here, Lana has added visual interest to the journaling by layering it onto multiple labels and tags. Cluster elements around your journaling to add depth to the layout without losing the negative space (open area in the top right) that "frames" the journaling as the focus of the page.

Supplies: Cardstock, patterned paper (Prima); chipboard stickers (K&Co.); brads (Making Memories); card (Fancy Pants); flower (Prima); journaling tabs (Heidi Swapp); transparency (My Mind's Eye); Misc: ink

When working with sketches, think of them as jumping off points. Here, I've turned the sketch 90° and then flipped it horizontally. A sketch should be used as inspiration to get you moving in the right direction and spark ideas but not to dictate where every little piece of the layout should go.

Supplies: Patterned paper (Fancy Pants, Rouge de Garance); felt accents, letter sticker (American Crafts); flowers (Blueye Dezines); transparency (Hambly); adhesive (Scrapbook Adhesive by 3L); Misc: brads, ink, pen

creative *sparks*

When you have a large amount of journaling, consider creating your layout right down to the last element, and then adding the journaling into the open space on the layout. This will accent your design while still giving you plenty of room to tell your story.

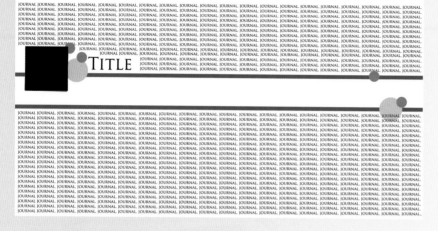

Creating a two-page layout is an excellent way to add lots of room for extensive journaling. Use this sketch as a starting point, but don't feel you have to include as much journaling as shown. This sketch also allows plenty of room for additional photos or ephemera.

Pictured here is Grandma & Grandpa on their wedding day. Their lives together just beginning. I wonder what their dreams for their future together were on that day. I wonder if they dreamt of having children & Grandpa running the family company with his brothers one day. Probably but as we all know life has a way of changing the path we think we are on. They did have children together. Four girls in fact, who all grew up healthy & happy but the future of the company was not what they expected. It folded & that set their lives on a completely different path. It caused them to move towns four times as   Grandpa tried to find

work. Their lives were hard but Grandma eventually ran a successful rooming house in Sarnia, ON where they remained until they died. It is funny to look at what their dreams might have been & know how differently their lives together turned out.

JACK and IRENE

January 3, 1955

Artwork: Crystal Jeffrey Rieger

On this layout, Crystal added this wonderful heart shape to the sketch to symbolize her grandparents' love. The bright white immediately draws your eye to the photo and the title. The horizontal band in the sketch helps to move your eye across the page and into the journaling. Remember when approaching a two-page layout to view the pages as one large canvas, continuing elements like shapes, titles or patterned paper across the gutter for a pleasing display that truly does your ancestors' photos justice.

Supplies: Cardstock (Bazzill, Paper Company); patterned paper (American Crafts); acrylic letters, snowflake accents (Heidi Swapp); adhesive (Scrapbook Adhesive by 3L); Misc: pen, photo corners

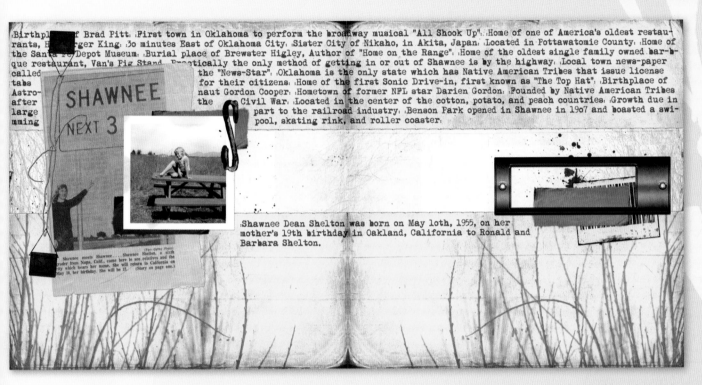

When you have large amounts of journaling to add to a layout, consider organizing it in a decorative way so that it almost becomes part of the pattern of the page. For this layout, I wanted to include a number of facts about the town my mom was named after. I added them to the page with two sets of colons in between each fact, allowing the list to span horizontally across the entire width of the two pages to enhance the design of the page.

Supplies: Software (Adobe); digital embellishments, patterned paper, tag by Melgen Designs (Oscraps); letters by Michelle Coleman (Little Dreamer)

creative*sparks*

If you are looking for a bit more information to add to a layout, try conducting a search at Wikipedia (www.wikipedia.com). Wikipedia is a free online encyclopedia with more information on more topics than you could ever think of. Give it a try!

Focus on Photos

As I've researched my family history, I've come across many wonderful photos that I can't find any information about. While it's important to always search out the story behind the photo, sometimes a photo will have to speak for itself. In these instances, make the photo the main focus of the page and choose colors, papers and embellishments that enhance the photo without distracting from it. Then choose an appropriate title that conveys the mood of the shot.

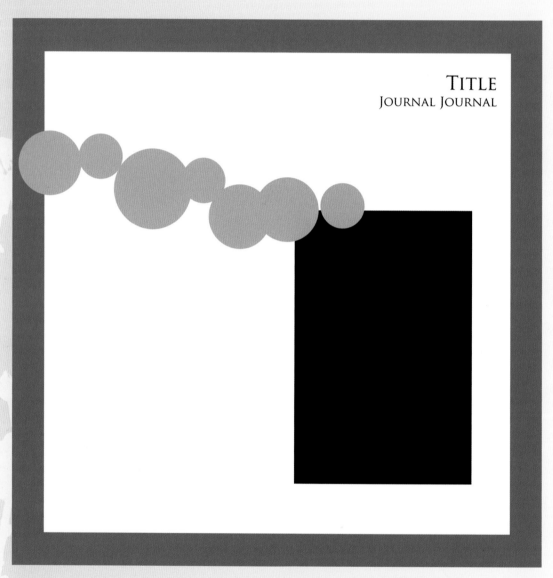

TITLE
JOURNAL JOURNAL

Try this sketch as a jumpstart for composing a page that focuses on your photo.
Surrounding the photo with lots of white space really allows it to pop off the page.

Apparently

the siGN

was not quite large enough

DO NOT
FEED THE
BEARS

Artwork: Erin Derkatz

This photo is so amazing, how could you not let it take center stage? This photo tells a wonderful story all on its own. By enhancing it with colors and minimal journaling, Erin has allowed it to be the primary focus of the page.

Supplies: Cardstock (Bazzill); patterned paper (Cosmo Cricket, Scenic Route); rub-ons (Autumn Leaves); Misc: pen

SUE

AT FIFTEEN

Use a white background and minimal embellishments to let your photo take center stage. For a bit of added interest, tear 1" (3cm) of each side of the white cardstock, using a ruler as a straight edge, then mount the page onto a colored cardstock background. Allow your embellishments to spill off the edge of the white onto the backing piece for added depth and dimension.

Supplies: Cardstock (Bazzill, WorldWin); labels (Dymo); rhinestone (Prima); stamps (Sugarloaf); adhesive (Scrapbook Adhesive by 3L, Therm O Web); ink (Ranger)

creative *techniques*

Stamping an Image

You'd be surprised at how a simple stamp can make a powerful statement on a layout. Try this technique when you would like an elegant yet understated look on your page.

Materials

- Rubber stamp
- Ink
- White or neutral cardstock
- Scissors
- Dimensional adhesive

1 Stamp your image onto white or neutral cardstock, leaving enough space between stamping for cutting.

2 Trim around each image, leaving a small border. This allows you to have less-than-perfect cuts without making your mistakes obvious.

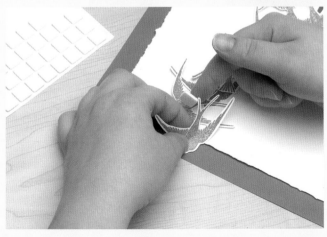

3 Arrange the cut images on your layout in a way that suits you, then carefully lift one piece and adhere it to the page with dimensional adhesive. Continue with the remaining pieces until you are finished. Vary whether you place each successive image above or below the previous image to keep the display from becoming repetitive.

JOURNAL JOURNAL
JOURNAL JOURNAL
TITLE

This is a very simple and traditional sketch that leaves a lot of room for personalization. Keep frills and embellishments to a minimum—just enough to balance the page—so the focus remains on the photo.

Frank A. Sampson
WWI 1917

When using a sketch for inspiration, try to make it a jumping-off point and then personalize the layout to make it your own. Here, I turned the photo at an angle and tore the edges of the horizontal patterned paper to soften the stiff pose of the photo subject. Try placing a frame offset around an area of your photo that you would like to further highlight, like the subject's face or hands.

Supplies: Cardstock (WorldWin); patterned paper (American Crafts, Prima); stamps (Gel-a-tins); rub-ons (Hambly); ribbon (SEI); frame (Prima); brad (Bazzill); adhesive (Duck, Therm O Web); Misc: ink

Artwork: Cindy Ellen Russell

Who could pass up an amazing photo like this one? Cindy enhanced the mystique of this photo of her mother at Stonehenge by accenting it with photos of space downloaded from the NASA Web site. The strength and vertical lines in the photo are even more striking because all other lines on the layout are curved. Cindy expanded on the ovals in the sketch by creating curved lines with patterned paper that draw the eye directly into the strong lines of the photo.

Supplies: Cardstock (Bazzill); patterned paper (Karen Foster, KI Memories, Me & My Big Ideas, Sandylion, Urban Lily); transparency (K&Co.); chipboard (BasicGrey, Maya Road); clock accents (7gypsies, Bazzill, Heidi Swapp, Paperbilities); stamp (Technique Tuesday); Misc: brad, chalk, ink, pen

Another way to make the photo the main focus of the page is to hide the journaling. This way the only things on the page are colors and patterns that enhance your wonderful photos. There are many ways to hide journaling. Be creative about where you place it—beneath a photo, beneath an element, or tucked into an envelope—and you'll add even more interest and dimension to your page.

Supplies: Cardstock (WorldWin); patterned paper (American Craft, Daisy D's, SEI); hinges (Daisy D's); adhesive (Scrapbook Adhesives by 3L); ink (Ranger); Misc: colored pencils, pen

Concealing Journaling

Hiding journaling on your page is a fun and interesting way to add more of a story without taking up precious design space. Once you have the basic idea down, you can begin to hide journaling in many creative places.

Materials

- Cardstock
- Hinges with matching brads
- Patterned paper
- Archival pen

1   Cut your patterned paper to the desired size. Make sure it is large enough to fit your journaling beneath but small enough to fit in the space you've allotted for it on your lay-out. Use distress ink to ink the edges of the paper.

2   Cut a journaling block from white or neutral covered cardstock in the same size and shape as the cover piece. Attach this piece to your layout and add the desired journaling.

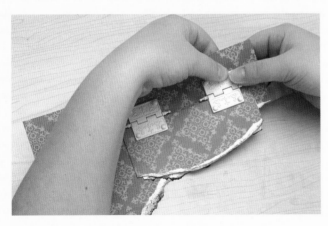

3   Line up one side of each hinge on the cover piece so that the flat part is flush with the paper but the round middle part of the hinge does not overlap it. Use a paper piercer to make a hole through each hole in the hinge, then attach it with your matching brads.

4   Lay the cover piece with hinges on top of the journaling block, lining it up exactly. Pierce the layout with the paper piercer through each remaining hole in the hinges. Use brads to attach the top of the hinges to the layout.

She Looks Oh So mod

Artwork: Cindy Ellen Russell

Try to think outside the box when creating hidden journaling, or other secret elements on your page. Here Cindy has added an entirely new dimension to her page with hidden journaling. At first glance you'd never even know that there was something wonderful tucked inside. As you can see, Cindy has used the space created by the hidden pocket not only for more journaling but to continue to enhance the design from the rest of the page. The pop-up embellishment is an extra-special touch.

Supplies: Cardstock (Bazzill); patterned paper (Fancy Pants); rub-ons (American Crafts, Autumn Leaves, Doodlebug); chipboard letters (Maya Road); label (Paper Source); stamp (Autumn Leaves); postcard (Paperchase); Misc: colored pencils, gel medium, glitter, ink, paint, pens

Artwork: Erin Derkatz

Hidden journaling doesn't have to be reserved only for instances when you have a lot to say and not a lot of space to say it in. It can also be used for times when you want to keep a sentiment private. Here, Erin uses the technique for a simple handwritten note that she easily keeps out of sight behind a small piece of green paper topped with a dandelion transparency. Try using a simple brad to tack a piece of paper over a short note so it pivots easily.

Supplies: Cardstock (Bazzill); patterned paper (Bam Pop, KI Memories, Making Memories); stickers (7gypsies, Making Memories); decorative tape (Heidi Swapp, Making Memories); ribbon (BasicGrey); rub-ons (Hambly); brad (Cactus Pink)

creative *sparks*

Just because you are scrapping your family heritage doesn't mean you can't also combine current feelings and photos. Remember that your childhood and current family relationships are just as important as those that happened in the past, and they have just as important a place in scrapbooks about your family legacy.

Put It Together

In this album, I've combined all of the techniques from this chapter and repeated subtle design elements on each page to create a cohesive album. When you are planning an album, choose a variety of colors to use throughout the book so that you are not limited on each individual page, but so that each page also flows nicely into the next.

Besides a cohesive color palette, a mini book should have a variety of design elements that relate each page in the album to the rest. In this album, I've chosen to use bird and owl images on each page. The images are a light cream color, and generally do not take center stage in the album, but definitely help create a cohesive feel as you flip through each page.

Supplies: Cardstock (WorldWin); patterned paper (Fontwerks, Hambly); letter stickers (American Crafts, BasicGrey); rub-ons, transparency (Hambly); chipboard scroll (Everlasting Keepsakes); adhesive (Elmer's, Scrapbook Adhesives by 3L, Therm O Web); Misc: acrylic paint, chain, eyelet, glitter

The principle of choosing a theme to create a cohesive album also applies when creating an individual page. This page is quite simple to create. Strategically placed rounded corners guide the eye around the page as well as relate the photo to the background paper.

To add some variation to a mini album, use a piece of transparency as your background instead of basic cardstock or patterned paper. Trim the transparency to the size you desire and round one of the corners for added interest. Adhere photos, paint, glitter, a rub-on image and any other embellishments that support your theme.

If you have even more journaling to add inside a small mini album like this one, try including a tiny accordion album within the book. There are many albums that can be made by hand-folding, including matchbook albums, traditional accordion albums and this fancy accordion album. Simply choose your favorite and shrink it down until it fits on your page.

creative *techniques*

Crafting an Origami Album

Creating this fancy album to place within a larger album or other altered project couldn't be easier. The folds can be a bit tricky at first, but once you get the hang of it, you'll be finding all sorts of new uses for this technique.

Materials

- Dry adhesive
- Cardstock
- Patterned paper
- Corner rounder (optional)

1 Trim one piece of patterned paper and two pieces of cardstock to 5" x 5" (13cm x 13cm).

2 For added interest, round all four of the corners of the paper.

3 Fold each piece of paper in half twice to form a cross. Then fold each piece on the diagonal once.

4 Align the top right corner of the patterned paper piece beneath the bottom left corner of one piece of cardstock. Diagonal folds should run parallel. Adhere. Align the bottom left corner of the piece of patterned paper beneath the top right corner of the remaining piece of cardstock. Diagonal folds should run parallel. Adhere.

5 Fold the piece so the squares stack on top of each other and the corners with the diagonal folds tuck in between them. The diagonally folded corners of the cardstock should tuck toward you; the diagonally folded corners of the patterned paper should fold away from you.

6 Attach a small ribbon to the back of the album and bring it around to the front to tie it closed. You may now adhere the tiny album into your larger album, layout or altered project.

the story so far...

A TALE OF PASSION
A TALE OF COURAGE
a love story

You made this house a home—

oure gonna get—forrest—com

Be Subtle—Be strong, go w

Ove as though you have ne

Resolved to having her

own **HOUSE**. Olga spent

endless hours salvaging

lumber and other scraps for

insulation. When the house was

refinished in the 70's, Gordon's

locks were found in the walls.

Eventual

work par

and Gor

their "N

there, de

to make

Chapter six

Adding Finishing Touches

By this point, I'm sure you've created some awesome pages that truly represent your family's story and your personality. You have pages full of life and color, ideas for fun albums and a new approach to scrapping your heritage photos. That means it's time to wrap things up. Literally.

Heritage pages and albums are perfect for gifts or for sharing at family get-togethers. There are many ways to bind scrapbook albums, from just slipping your completed pages into a pre-made album with page protectors to traditional hand-binding. You should choose your method of binding and presentation based on what you plan to do with the album. Whether it's a gift, will be on display in your home or will be added to as the years go by, there is a perfect finishing method for you—you just have to find it.

Bind Your Own Mini Albums

Albums can be created and bound many different ways. Of course, you can always start with a pre-bound mini album or add your pages to page protectors in a D-ring album, but an album put together solely by you will always be the most interesting and special.

Jump-ring albums provide complete freedom with page sizes and shapes. Here, I've used part of a manila folder covered with a scratch piece of paper torn from a journal as my background piece. By allowing the photo to extend off the page, following the lines in the scrap paper, the image becomes the central focus. This technique is made possible by the lack of restrictions of the jump-ring binding.

Supplies: Patterned paper (A2Z, CherryArte, Daisy D's); stamps (Sugarloaf); chipboard shapes (Everlasting Keepsakes); journaling accent, Kraft paper, rub-ons (Hambly); adhesive (Scrapbook Adhesive by 3L); ink (Ranger); Misc: book rings, colored pencils, floss, pen

creative*sparks*

For tags or pieces of ephemera that you'd like to have threaded onto only one jump ring, use the template to be sure the piece is not so large that it touches the second jump ring. Otherwise, the page will become damaged and may not lay flat.

Creating a 3-Ring Album Template

Binding an album with jump rings is quick and simple with a few preparations. First, you should decide how many rings you want to use: one, two, three or more. Then, you should choose whether the rings will be at the top of the album or at the side. This will depend mainly on the composition of the pages and the ephemera you would like to include in the album.

Materials

- Hole punch (anywhere punch or hand punch)
- Scrap cardstock
- Ruler
- Pen or pencil

1 Using a scrap piece of cardstock and a ruler, measure in from the edge ½" (1.2cm) to 1" (2.5cm) and draw a line.

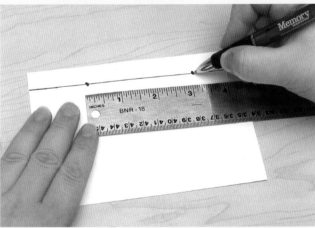

2 Mark two spots (more if you are using more rings) on your line 2" (5cm) to 4" (10cm) apart.

3 Use a hole punch to punch a hole at each mark. Use this handy template to mark the position of the holes on each page you'd like to include in your album. Then punch holes at the marks and thread jump rings, plastic book rings or ribbon through them.

For more variety, try throwing out the background altogether. Here, I've bound the photo directly to the jump rings, then embellished the photo with corners and a journaling spot.

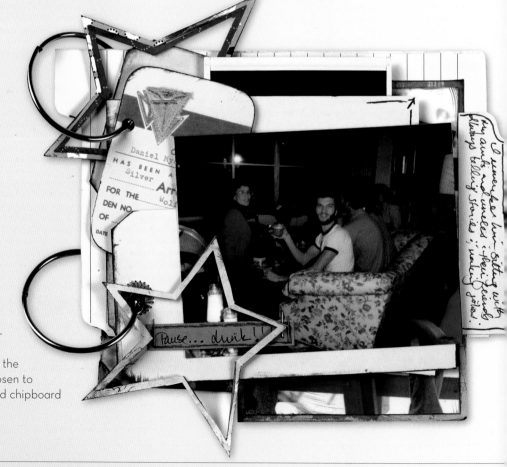

Also consider adding extra elements to the jump rings, either between pages or to decorate the rings themselves. Here, I've chosen to incorporate nesting star-shaped chipboard throughout the album.

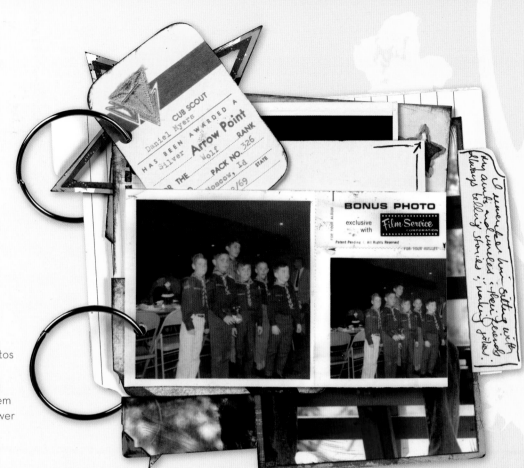

Include ephemera or memorabilia by grouping it with photos from the same time period or event. Stagger the photos and ephemera to allow for each item to be partially seen as the viewer flips through the album.

Treat each page as its own entity. Creating interest in each one individually will give your album variety and make it fun to flip through.

how
to
name

a grandparent

& other family
nonsense

Artwork: Crystal Jeffrey Rieger

Jump rings give you the ability to bind any combination of page
sizes and pieces of ephemera. They are inexpensive (generally less than a dollar
each depending on size), and they enable you to continue to add pages to your album as your
family story grows.

Supplies: Patterned paper (A2Z, Bo-Bunny, Polar Bear Press); letter stickers (Arctic Frog); felt (Blueye Dezines); adhesive (Scrapbook Adhesive
by 3L); Misc: book rings, cardboard, paint, pen

It seems to me that our families have come up with some rather bizarre names for the grandparents in our family. There was Grummy & Grumpy... oh & Gardie too...

Well you get the idea. Read on to decide for yourself.

an intro

P! every book needs one...

Be creative when choosing the materials for your albums. Here, Crystal has chosen cardboard as the base for her album, giving it a playful feel that matches her theme and adding tons of texture.

Hildegard (Graft) Scott

Faye (Scott) Rieger

Austin Rieger

grummy

apparently grummy started with Katie. she mistakenly combined the two names — mommy & grandma and a new name was born. it was just so cute & funny that it stuck!

Gift Your Albums

Handmade mini albums make quick and easy gifts and can be quite elegant. Once you learn the basic techniques for creating these albums in a couple of different styles, you'll be able to alter the process to give your album a custom look.

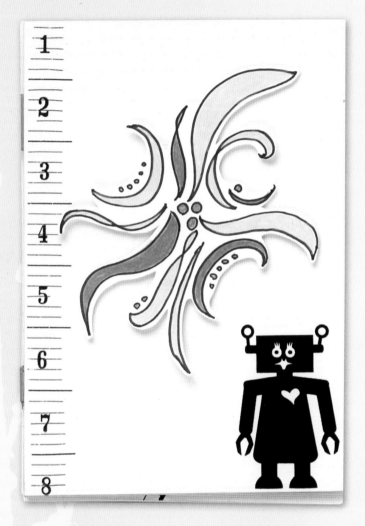

The cover of your album should give a little hint as to what's inside. I chose the ruler rub-on because all of the photos contained within are school portraits. The funky robot, hand-doodling and fun colors hint at the themes used throughout the album. For this album, I combined a school portrait of each member of one generation of my family as a gift for my grandmother.

Supplies: Cardstock (WorldWin); chipboard mats (Die Cuts with a View); rub-ons (Hambly); transparency (3M); stamps (Gel-a-tins); ribbon (Fancy Pants); adhesive (Scrapbook Adhesive by 3L, Therm O Web); Misc: colored pencils, ink, pen

Printable transparencies make fast work of titles, especially when you need multiple titles that coordinate. Download free fonts online to add the perfect touch. Sites like Linotype (www.linotype.com) and DaFont (www.dafont.com) are good places to look. If you really want to get wild, you can add a few digital brushes to your title before printing it.

Making a Chipboard Album

Family mini albums make awesome gifts for just about any occasion. As you gather photos and stories together, think about how they relate to each other. Once you have a group of photos you like, combine them into this quick and simple album for a fun gift.

Materials

- Chipboard mat boards, (twice as many boards as you would like to have pages)
- Two strips of ribbon (length in inches = 4 times the total number of pages)
- One 10" (25cm) strip of ribbon
- Scrapbook adhesives photo tape

1 Lay half your total number of mat boards down side by side. Space them about ⅛" (1.9cm) apart.

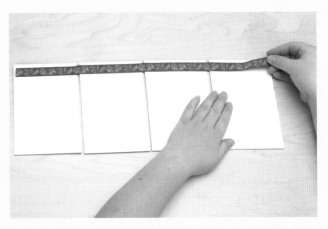

2 Use photo tape to attach the first row of ribbon, about ¼" (6.4mm) from the top. Repeat with the second row of ribbon, about ¼" (6.4mm) from the bottom. Pull the ribbon straight and taut between each successive board.

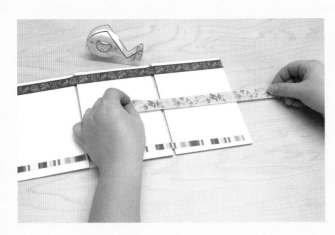

3 Adhere the 10" (25cm) strip of ribbon across the center of the right board. Tuck the excess ribbon on the left side of the board beneath the adjacent page.

4 Ball up small pieces of the photo tape with your fingers and attach a second mat board on top of the ribbon. Line each mat board up evenly with the one below it. Fold up your album accordion-style and bring each side of the 10" (25cm) ribbon around to the front to tie closed.

Fold an accordion album out of a few basic pieces of patterned paper to create a simple but stunning gift. Albums made of patterned paper are quick and easy because you probably always all have the materials you need on hand. This album is made simply by connecting two 12" x 12" (30cm x 30cm) patterned papers at one edge, then folding it in half, creating a pocket up on each side and then folding it into an accordion. Play around with a few scrap pieces of patterned paper to find a style you like.

Supplies: Cardstock (Bazzill); patterned paper (Chatterbox, Crate Paper, Once Upon a Doodle); decorative tape, rub-ons (7gypsies); iron-on (Hewlett Packard); rhinestones (K&Co.); ribbon (American Crafts, Heidi Swapp); buttons (Autumn Leaves); adhesive (EK Success); Misc: pen, thread

Artwork: Erin Derkatz

Using tags in a mini album nearly doubles your space for journaling and pictures. Here, Erin turned her pictures into tags and tucked them into the album. She was then free to use the album itself for her journaling. This approach also ensures that the viewer will really give the album the attention it deserves by making it an interactive experience.

creative*sparks*

Remember that the title of your album gives your readers the first impression of what to expect when they open it up. Choose something that fits the subject matter inside but that is also intriguing. One-word titles are often strong and confident, whereas multi-word titles can be poetic. It often helps to work on the cover after you've completed the interior of the album. Spend some time brainstorming and give yourself permission to step outside the box.

Alter Album Covers

Try altering the covers of pre-made albums. If you plan to add pages over time, purchase an album with page protectors. There are many unique albums on the market today that focus on a central theme or story. With these, you can create directly on the provided pages and tear out any extras you don't plan to fill.

Artwork: Lana Rappette

Altering a pre-made album cover is a quick and easy way to add a personal touch to a heritage album without going through the process of cutting pages and binding. Finding the right mood can be as simple as choosing the right piece of patterned paper. Here, Lana removed the cover from the album (use a screwdriver to remove the screws—just remember to put them in a safe place while you work!) and then gave it a quick base coat in acrylic paint. The patterned paper covering the front is cut to size and slit at the spine and diagonally across the window. The result is a stunning album that truly represents the stories held inside.

Supplies: Album (Making Memories): patterned paper (K&Co.); rub-ons (Hambly, K&Co.); card (Fancy Pants); flowers (Prima); rhinestones (Doodlebug); stamp (Fontwerks); adhesive (Aleene's); Misc: glitter

Matchbook album kits come in many different colors and patterns and are quick and easy to put together. Although they come in a pre-coordinated kit, you can see that with a little creativity, you can easily make this type of album your own. A variety of textures makes the inside of the album almost irresistible.

Supplies: Matchbook album (BasicGrey); cardstock (Bazzill); fabric tape (Making Memories); rub-ons (Autumn Leaves); stamps (K&Co., Stampin' Up); adhesive (Elmer's); Misc: ink, thread

Artwork: Erin Derkatz

Artwork: Cindy Ellen Russell

Consider altering an album that holds CDs or DVDs. For a digital scrapper, this is a great way to share all of your family history layouts without having to print multiple copies. For a traditional scrapper, this is an excellent way to compile family photos, stories and information as you find it, so it will be easily organized and safe.

Supplies: Cardstock (Bazzill, Paperbilities); patterned paper (Making Memories); chipboard letters (EK Success); ribbon (Wrights); stamps (Hero Arts); Misc: ink

GRANDMA MARY JANE

GRANDPA FRANK

ROBERT ROSS

UNCLE BILL

UNCLE JIM

UNCLE DAVE

RUSSELL PHOTOS ★

Fabric is fun to use as an album cover, as it adds a whole new dimension of color and texture. Vintage fabrics can be purchased online and are a great canvas to begin your heritage album cover. In addition, many rub-ons will adhere easily to fabric, as will a variety of inks if you'd like to try stamping.

Supplies: Album (Paper Wished); chipboard (Zsiage); button (JHB); stamps (Gel-a-tins); rub-ons, transparency (Hambly); adhesive (Scrapbook Adhesive by 3L, Therm O Web); Misc: ink, thread

creative *techniques*

Covering an Album with Fabric

An easy way to quickly cover a pre-made album is to use fabric. With a few quick measurements and a little patience, you can make a bold cover that will also withstand the usual handling that an album endures.

Materials

- Album
- Fabric
- Pencil
- Measuring tape
- Craft knife
- Iron
- Dry adhesive
- Various embellishments

1 Open the album over the fabric and use a pencil to trace around the outside edges.

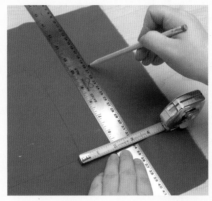

2 Remove the album and measure another 3" (8cm) from the sides and 1" (2.5cm) from the top and bottom. Use a craft knife to cut out the resulting rectangle.

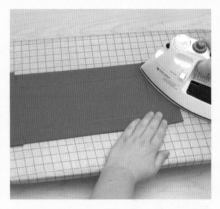

3 Fold 1" (2.5cm) of fabric down from the top and bottom of the rectangle along the pencil lines, and iron to set the crease. Repeat this step with the sides.

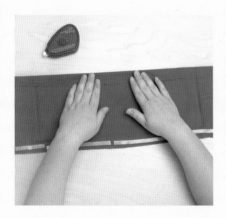

4 Run dry adhesive along all the top and bottom of the rectangle, then fold them over and press firmly. Repeat with each of the two remaining sides.

5 You will have formed two pockets at each edge of the fabric. Tuck each end of your album into each of the pockets to ensure a good fit.

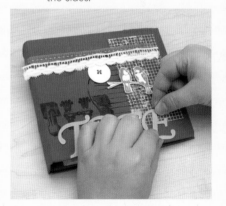

6 Decorate cover as desired.

sourceguide

3L Corporation
(800) 828-3130
www.scrapbook-adhesives.com

3M
(888) 364-3577
www.3m.com

7gypsies
(877) 749-7797
www.sevengypsies.com

A2Z Essentials
(419) 663-2869
www.geta2z.com

Adornit/Carolee's Creations
(435) 563-1100
www.adornit.com

Aitoh Company
(800) 681-5533
www.aitoh.com

Aleene's - see Duncan

American Crafts
(801) 226-0747
www.americancrafts.com

American Traditional Designs
(800) 448-6656
www.americantraditional.com

ANW Crestwood
(973) 406-5000
www.anwcrestwood.com

Arctic Frog
(479) 636-3764
www.arcticfrog.com

Autumn Leaves
(800) 588-6707
www.autumnleaves.com

Avery Dennison Corporation
(800) 462-8379
www.avery.com

BAM POP LLC
www.bampop.com

BasicGrey
(801) 544-1116
www.basicgrey.com

Bazzill Basics Paper
(480) 558-8557
www.bazzillbasics.com

Blueye Dezines
(917) 596-4837
www.blueyedezines.com.au

Bo-Bunny Press
(801) 771-4010
www.bobunny.com

Cactus Pink
(866) 798-2446
www.cactuspink.com

CatScrap
www.catscrap.com

Cavallini Papers & Co., Inc.
(800) 226-5287
www.cavallini.com

Chatterbox, Inc.
(208) 461-5077
www.chatterboxinc.com

CherryArte
(212) 465-3495
www.cherryarte.com

Chronicle Books
(800) 722-6657
www.chroniclebooks.com

Cloud 9 Design
(866) 348-5661
www.cloud9design.biz

Colorbök, Inc.
(800) 366-4660
www.colorbok.com

Cosmo Cricket
(800) 852-8810
www.cosmocricket.com

Crafter's Workshop, The
(877) 272-3837
www.thecraftersworkshop.com

Crate Paper
(801) 798-8996
www.cratepaper.com

Crayola
(800) 272-9652
www.crayola.com

Creative Imaginations
(800) 942-6487
www.cigift.com

Daisy D's Paper Company
(888) 601-8955
www.daisydspaper.com

Darice, Inc.
(800) 321-1494
www.darice.com

Dèjá Views
(800) 243-8419
www.dejaviews.com

Die Cuts With A View
(801) 224-6766
www.diecutswithaview.com

Digital Paper Tearing
www.digitalpapertearing.com

Digital Scrapbook Artisan Guild
www.dsaguild.com

Digital Scrapbook Place, The
(866) 396-6906
www.digitalscrapbookplace.com

Do You Digi?
www.doyoudigi.com

Doodlebug Design Inc.
(877) 800-9190
www.doodlebug.ws

Duck Products - see Henkel

Duncan Enterprises
(800) 438-6226
www.duncanceramics.com

Dymo
(800) 426-7827
www.dymo.com

EK Success, Ltd.
(800) 524-1349
www.eksuccess.com

Elmer's Products, Inc.
(800) 848-9400
www.elmers.com

E-Scape and Scrap
www.e-scapeandscrap.net

Everlasting Keepsakes
(816) 896-7037
www.everlastingkeepsakes.com

Fancy Pants Designs, LLC
(801) 779-3212
www.fancypantsdesigns.com

Fiskars, Inc.
(866) 348-5661
www.fiskars.com

Fontwerks
(604) 942-3105
www.fontwerks.com

Frances Meyer, Inc.
(413) 584-5446
www.francesmeyer.com

Gel-a-tins
(800) 393-2151
www.gelatinstamps.com

Hallmark Cards, Inc.
(800) 425-5627
www.hallmark.com

Hambly Studios
(800) 451-3999
www.hamblystudios.com

Heidi Grace Designs, Inc.
(866) 348-5661
www.heidigrace.com

Heidi Swapp/Advantus Corporation
(904) 482-0092
www.heidiswapp.com

Henkel Consumer Adhesives, Inc.
(800) 321-0253
www.stickwithhenkel.com

Hero Arts Rubber Stamps, Inc.
(800) 822-4376
www.heroarts.com

Hewlett-Packard Company
www.hp.com/go/scrapbooking

Imaginisce
(801) 908-8111
www.imaginisce.com

Inkadinkado Rubber Stamps
(800) 523-8452
www.inkadinkado.com

Innovative Storage Designs, Inc.
(262) 241-3749
www.innovative-storage.com

It Takes Two
(800) 331-9843
www.ittakestwo.com

JHB International
(800) 525-9007
www.buttons.com

Junkitz
(732) 792-1108
www.junkitz.com

K&Company
(888) 244-2083
www.kandcompany.com

Karen Foster Design
(801) 451-9779
www.karenfosterdesign.com

KI Memories
(972) 243-5595
www.kimemories.com

Kodomo, Inc.
(650) 685-1828
www.kodomoinc.com

Lee Products
(800) 989-3544
www.leeproducts.com

Li'l Davis Designs
(480) 223-0080
www.lildavisdesigns.com

Little Black Dress Designs
(360) 897-8844
www.littleblackdressdesigns.com

Little Dreamer Designs
www.littledreamerdesigns.com

Luxe Designs
(972) 573-2120
www.luxedesigns.com

Magic Mesh
(651) 345-6374
www.magicmesh.com

Magic Scraps
(904) 482-0092
www.magicscraps.com

Making Memories
(801) 294-0430
www.makingmemories.com

May Arts
(800) 442-3950
www.mayarts.com

Maya Road, LLC
(877) 427-7764
www.mayaroad.com

me & my BiG ideas
(949) 583-2065
www.meandmybigideas.com

Melissa Frances/Heart & Home, Inc.
(888) 616-6166
www.melissafrances.com

Michaels Arts & Crafts
(800) 642-4235
www.michaels.com

Midori
(800) 659-3049
www.midoriribbon.com

My Mind's Eye, Inc.
(800) 665-5116
www.mymindseye.com

My Sentiments Exactly
(719) 260-6001
www.sentiments.com

Once Upon a Scribble
(435) 628-8577
www.onceuponascribble.com

One Heart...One Mind, LLC
(888) 414-3690

Oscraps
www.oscraps.com

Paper Accents
(800) 291-9758
www.paperaccents.com

Paper Company, The -
see ANW Crestwood

Paper Salon
(800) 627-2648
www.papersalon.com

Paper Source
(888) 727-3711
www.paper-source.com

Paper Wishes by Hot Off the Press
(888) 300-3406
www.paperwishes.com

Paperbilities - no source available

Paperchase
www.paperchase.co.uk

Papier Valise
(403) 277-1802
www.papiervalise.com

Petaloo
(800) 458-0350
www.petaloo.com

Piggy Tales
(702) 755-8600
www.piggytales.com

Plaid Enterprises, Inc.
(800) 842-4197
www.plaidonline.com

Polar Bear Press
(801) 451-7670
www.polarbearpress.com

Pressed Petals
(801) 224-6766
www.pressedpetals.com

Prima Marketing, Inc.
(909) 627-5532
www.primamarketinginc.com

Purple Onion Designs
www.purpleoniondesigns.com

Queen & Co.
(858) 613-7858
www.queenandcompany.com

Ranger Industries, Inc.
(800) 244-2211
www.rangerink.com

Rouge de Garance
www.rougedegarance.com

Rusty Pickle
(801) 746-1045
www.rustypickle.com

Sandylion Sticker Designs
(800) 387-4215
www.sandylion.com

Sassafras Lass
(801) 269-1331
www.sassafraslass.com

Sausan Designs
www.sausandesigns.com

Scenic Route Paper Co.
(801) 542-8071
www.scenicroutepaper.com

ScrapArtist
(734) 717-7775
www.scrapartist.com

Scrapbook Adhesives by 3L
www.scrapbook-adhesives.com

Scrapbook Graphics
www.scrapbookgraphics.com

Scrapbook Sally
(866) 727-2559
www.scrapbooksally.com

SEI, Inc.
(800) 333-3279
www.shopsei.com

Shabby Shoppe, The
www.theshabbyshoppe.com

Stampin' Up!
(800) 782-6787
www.stampinup.com

Staples, Inc.
www.staples.com

Stemma/Masterpiece Studios
www.masterpiecestudios.com

Strano Designs
(508) 888-3189
www.stranodesigns.com

Sugarloaf Products, Inc.
(770) 484-0722
www.sugarloafproducts.com

Swarovski
(800) 426-3088
www.swarovski.com

Sweetwater
(800) 359-3094
www.sweetwaterscrapbook.com

Technique Tuesday, LLC
(503) 644-4073
www.techniquetuesday.com

Therm O Web, Inc.
(800) 323-0799
www.thermoweb.com

Tombow
(800) 835-3232
www.tombowusa.com

Urban Lily
www.urbanlily.com

U.S. Stamp & Sign
(800) 347-1044
www.usstamp.com

We R Memory Keepers, Inc.
(801) 539-5000
www.weronthenet.com

Windgefleuster Designs - no
source available

WorldWin Papers
(888) 834-6455
www.worldwinpapers.com

Wrights Ribbon Accents
(877) 597-4448
www.wrights.com

Zsiage, LLC
(718) 224-1976
www.zsiage.com

Ztampf
www.ztampf.com

Artists

Learn more about the talented women who contributed their amazing artwork to the creation of this book.

Ronee Parsons lives in Olympia, Washington with her husband, son and a group of furry four-legged companions. Ronee has dabbled in many different art forms since childhood. She started scrapping in 2004 as a way to document her son's early years and quickly grew passionate about the art. She truly enjoys finding the stories from everyday life and capturing them using a combination of words, colors and images. Ronee is a 2007 Memory Makers Master and maintains a blog at www.roneeparsons.blogspot.com.

Karen Bowers lives in northern California with her husband and two sons. Karen has wanted to be an artist since childhood, and her wish came true with the birth of digital scrapbooking. The mixture of storytelling with images makes scrapbooking an ongoing passion and delight. Heritage scrapping offers Karen the opportunity to get to know her family's ancestors. Karen maintains a blog at http://karensdreamingbig.blogspot.com.

Erin Derkatz resides with her husband and daughter in Alberta, Canada, but dreams of living in a tropical rainforest. Erin's passions include deep conversation, vibrant color, being active, traveling to new places, good food, good books, sunny weather, collecting recipes and finding treasures. She loves to "make stuff" and, thus, regularly makes big creative messes. On occasion, Erin helps her husband at their natural health center. She likes shopping at the farmer's market and gets very excited about organic vegetables. Her closet is full of jeans and t-shirts, and she still wears a pair of brown leather boots she acquired in twelfth grade.

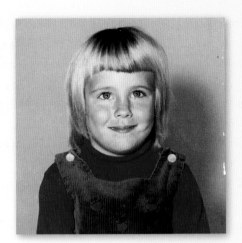

Catherine Feegel-Erhardt lives in Florida with her husband and three children. She describes her love of scrapbooking as an "addiction to paper and glue." She has been scrapbooking for three years, was awarded the title of Memory Makers Master in 2007 and is also an accomplished scrapbook teacher. In a past life, she worked as a registered nurse, despite her self-proclaimed germaphobic tendencies. Learn more about Catherine and her work on her blog at www.creativeondemad.typepad.com.

Lana Rappette is a creative, sometimes complicated, Michigan girl living a wonderfully content, simple life. She is married with three children all under the age of five. They are the reasons Lana began scrapbooking, and she couldn't be more grateful. Lana scrapbooks to remember her personal memories as well as the great tales of her family. She believes that passing down stories from generation to generation builds family pride. Lana is a stay-at-home mom raising her family and recording what she learns.

Crystal Jeffrey Rieger lives in Canada with her husband and two kids on a beautiful horse farm. She has always had an interest in art and trained in it for many years before moving on to the world of fashion. After the birth of her son, she decided to stay at home and search for an outlet for her creativity. She soon discovered scrapbooking, and it was love at first sight. In 2007 she won a spot on the Memory Makers Masters roster and has been happily creating and writing ever since. Crystal wrote her first book, Cut Loose: Break the Rules of Scrapbooking, to be published 2008. She maintains a blog at www.memorymakersmagazine.com/crystaljeffreyrieger.

Cindy Ellen Russell lives in Honolulu where she and her steady boyfriend work as staff photographers for the Honolulu Star-Bulletin. She began scrapbooking in 2003 upon the birth of their daughter, Cheo, and hasn't stopped since. She finds inspiration in the everyday of her native isles—from the rusty neon shop signs along King Street to the rugged, lush terrain of the Ko'olau Range. She is thankful for the love of her family, morning cuddles with her daughter, the safe comfort of her friends and the kindness of others.

Katrina Simeck is a California girl trying to stay warm in Vermont. She's wife to Rob and mom to Hope and Austin. By day she works as a project manager for a cosmetics manufacturer. After becoming overwhelmed with the notion of getting everything scrapped, Katrina put down paper and scissors for a few years. When she finally dusted off her supplies, she decided to throw out all the "rules" and instead focus on telling stories and capturing memories. The daughter of a writer and a photographer, Katrina has great resources for old photos and family history. She hopes her scrapbooks will give her loved ones a glimpse into the life of this 30-something, coffee-drinking, SUV-driving soccer mom who still listens to really loud music and has far too much patterned paper.

Michele Skinner began scrapbooking in 2000, following the birth of her son and trying in vain to find baby books that weren't covered with cartoon characters. Since then, the "baby booking" has taken on a life of its own. She discovered the true meaning of her scrapbooks is in the photos and stories, and everything else is just showing off. Submitting and getting published were occasional selfish indulgences, but when Michele was named a Memory Makers Master in 2007 she realized that maybe other people liked her photos and stories, too. She lives in Minnesota with her favorite scrap subjects: husband/geek Marc, son/genius Henry and daughter/comedienne Harper.

Index

Discover more modern ways to whip up amazing scrapbook layouts and other memory projects with these titles from Memory Makers Books!

Show it Off!

With tons of out-of-album project ideas—like shadow boxes, mini albums and photo cubes—plus step-by-step instructions for different techniques, *Show it Off!* gives you the tools for putting your creativity on display.

ISBN-13: 978-1-59963-025-0
ISBN-10: 1-59963-025-7
Paperback
128 pages
Z1937

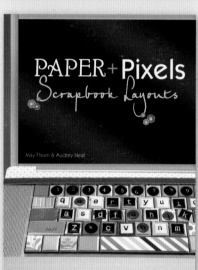

Paper + Pixels

With 40 digital techniques like making photo collages, editing photos, mixing digital papers, adding filters to text, creating embellishments, layering text and photos and more, *Paper + Pixels* is your guide to the exciting world of hybrid scrapbooking.

ISBN-13: 978-1-892127-93-8
ISBN-10: 1-892127-93-8
Paperback
128 pages
Z0350

Get It Scrapped!

Find everything you need to know for organizing your photos, analyzing what you have and making a plan for the layouts you'd like to create right here in *Get It Scrapped!*

ISBN-13: 978-1-59963-015-1
ISBN-10: 1-59963-015-X
Paperback
128 pages
Z1597

These books and other fine Memory Makers titles are available at your local scrapbook or craft retailer, bookstore or from online suppliers. Visit www.mycraftivity.com and www.memorymakersmagazine.com for more information.